Thrifty Main Dishes

Budget-Wise Dinners That Are Winners

MARGARET HAPPEL

Butterick Publishing

The author and publisher thank the following for supplying props for use in the photography: La Cuisinière, 867 Madison Ave., New York, NY 10021; Manhattan Ad Hoc Housewares, 842 Lexington Ave., New York, NY 10021; The Pottery Barn, 321 Tenth Ave., New York, NY 10011; and Villeroy and Boch, 41 Madison Avenue, New York, NY 10010.

Book Design: *Betty Binns*

Photography: *Bill Helms*

Pictured on the front cover: Porkburger-Apple-Potato Platter (page 48).

Library of Congress Cataloging in Publication Data

Happel, Margaret.
  Thrifty main dishes.

  Includes index.
  1. Cookery (Entries)   I. Title.
TX740.H278   641.8′2   79-15215
ISBN 0-88421-090-1

Manufactured and printed in the United States of America, published simultaneously in the USA and Canada.

CONTENTS

INTRODUCTION 5

1 Beef   7

2 Pork, Ham and Sausage   33

3 Veal and Lamb   55

4 Variety Meats   73

5 Poultry and Seafood   83

6 Meatless (Beans, Pasta, Rice,
    Eggs and Cheese)   109

INDEX 133

Introduction

You're in for a big surprise. You're about to find out that thrifty means tasty. Thrifty means variety. Thrifty means creating tempting, nutritious meals out of foods that are affordable.

People in other parts of the world have known this for a long time, and they've developed a fondness for their inexpensive national culinary treasures. Can you imagine the French without their onion soup, the Italians without their pasta, the Germans without their sausages?

Try a rump roast simmered in wine and spices until it's fork tender and swimming in rich, dark gravy, or delicate chicken sautéed with fresh orange and pecans. The imaginative recipes in this cookbook just might change your cooking—and shopping—habits forever.

Here are a few tips that will help you cut corners. You'll be surprised at how much you can save by adjusting your buying habits ever so slightly.

1. Buy in bulk whenever possible; it's usually cheaper. If you can learn to cut up your own meat, so much the better.

2. Keep a sharp eye out for store sales. They often spell big values. Comparison shopping can mean savings, too.

3. Use vegetable protein wisely; rice, beans and pasta are great meat extenders.

4. Make out a shopping list before you go to the supermarket. Resist impulse buying and avoid junk foods.

5. Buy jug wines for cooking. There are some pleasant Italian and California wines available in gallons and half-gallons.

By following these hints and making *Thrifty Main Dishes,* you can tackle your budget head-on and emerge well fed and happy.

Beef

If beef is your family's big favorite but it's putting the biggest squeeze on your food budget, welcome to the recipes in this chapter. Designed to make the most out of the more economical cuts, they offer happy alternatives to plain steaks and roasts.

Many old and new favorites are here: Belgian Beef Pot Roast, simmered in beer for extra zip; Chuck Steak Pizzaiola, flavored with green pepper, oregano and basil; Marinated London Broil, spectacular on a charcoal grill.

Of course, bottom round, rump and chuck require a bit more time for the slow-cooking methods that tenderize them. But properly prepared—simmered in wine with herbs and spices—they are actually tastier than the more expensive cuts. When buying roasts, remember that larger pieces of meat will not shrink or lose as much moisture during cooking as smaller ones. And larger roasts reheat nicely for a second or third meal, which saves you not only money but time.

Chuck and round steaks are excellent for marinating or pan braising with vegetables. Chuck is slightly tougher, but its even marbling of fat makes it more flavorful than round, which can dry out if not carefully cooked.

And what could be more of a budget booster than good old hamburger, especially when it's been transformed into imaginative dishes like Sweet-Sour Meatballs, Taco con Carne or, when you really want to wow them, Hamburger Wellington.

Ground chuck is your best buy in hamburger. Beware of unidentified ground beef, often tough scraps of meat loaded with fat—no bargain. Many supermarkets are experimenting with a combination of ground beef and soybean extender—pound for pound, an exceptional source of protein. If you wish, you can substitute this mix for ground beef in any of the recipes in this chapter.

With such a variety of recipes at your fingertips, you'll find it easy to enjoy beef while keeping your budget on an even keel.

Belgian Beef Pot Roast

3-pound rump roast
¼ cup flour
½ teaspoon garlic powder
¼ cup butter or margarine
2 tablespoons vegetable oil
4 cups sliced onions
one 12-ounce can beer
one 10½-ounce can beef broth
1 teaspoon sugar
1 teaspoon paprika
½ cup half-and-half or light cream

1. Wipe meat well with damp paper towels. Pat all surfaces of roast with mixture of flour and garlic powder to coat well.

2. Heat butter or margarine and oil in large saucepan or 6-quart Dutch oven over medium heat; add meat and brown on all sides, turning with wooden spoons to avoid piercing meat. Remove meat and set aside.

3. Add onions to drippings in pan; sauté until golden, about 5 minutes. Place meat on top of onions; add beer, beef broth, sugar and paprika. Bring liquid to simmering point; cover tightly.

4. Reduce heat to low; simmer for 2 hours or until meat is tender; add more beef broth if liquid level is low. Or cover tightly and bake at 300° F for 2 to 2½ hours, adding more broth if necessary. Just before serving, remove meat to warm serving platter and stir half-and-half or cream into pan juices; serve sauce alongside roast.

Serves 8.

Wine-Tender Pot Roast

3-pound rump roast
¼ cup flour
1 teaspoon salt
½ teaspoon pepper
¼ cup vegetable oil
1 cup chopped onion
one 10½-ounce can beef broth
1 cup dry red wine
2 cups diagonally sliced carrots, in ½-inch slices
2 cups diagonally sliced celery, in ½-inch slices

1. Wipe meat well with damp paper towels. Pat all surfaces of roast with mixture of flour, salt and pepper to coat well.

2. Heat oil in large saucepan or 6-quart Dutch oven over medium heat; add meat and brown on all sides, turning with wooden spoons to avoid piercing meat. Remove meat and set aside.

3. Add onion to drippings in pan; sauté until golden, about 5 minutes. Place meat on top of onion; add beef broth and red wine.

4. Reduce heat to low and simmer, covered, for 1¼ hours. Add carrots and celery; cover and simmer 45 minutes longer or until meat is tender, adding more wine if liquid level is low.

Serves 8.

Old-World Sauerbraten

2½-pound bottom round roast
1 cup red wine vinegar
1 cup water
1 cup sliced onion
⅓ cup brown sugar
¼ cup red wine
3 bay leaves, crumbled
½ cup flour
2 tablespoons vegetable oil
1 cup sour cream

1. Wipe beef well with damp paper towels. In large glass or pottery bowl, make marinade by blending vinegar, water, onion, brown sugar, red wine and bay leaves. Add meat; turn to coat well with marinade. Cover and chill for 24 hours, turning frequently. (The meat can be marinated for 2 to 3 days if desired.)

2. Remove meat from marinade; reserve marinade. Dredge meat well with flour, patting it into all surfaces.

3. Heat oil in large saucepan or Dutch oven over medium heat; add meat and brown on all sides. Add 3 cups marinade; bring to boiling point. Reduce heat to low and simmer, covered, for 2½ to 3 hours or until meat is tender. Remove meat to platter; keep warm.

4. Whisk sour cream into liquid; heat but do not boil. Serve alongside the meat.

Serves 8.

Note: For a thicker gravy, blend 2 tablespoons flour (or ¼ cup crushed gingersnaps) with 2 tablespoons water; stir into marinade after removing meat in step 3. Bring to boiling point to thicken before adding sour cream.

Chuck Steak Pizzaiola

2½- to 3-pound chuck steak, ¾ inch thick
2 tablespoons olive oil
1 cup chopped green pepper
1 clove garlic, crushed
two 8-ounce cans tomato sauce
1 teaspoon oregano
1 teaspoon basil

1. Wipe steak well with damp paper towels. Heat oil in large skillet over medium heat; add steak and sauté quickly to brown, about 2 minutes per side. Remove steak and set aside.

2. Add green pepper and garlic to drippings in skillet; sauté until pepper is tender, about 3 to 4 minutes. Stir in tomato sauce, oregano and basil; bring to simmering point.

3. Place meat in sauce. Reduce heat to low and simmer, covered, for 30 to 45 minutes or until meat is tender.

Serves 4.

Skillet Steak Sauté

2- to 2½-pound chuck steak,
½ inch thick
2 tablespoons vegetable oil
1 clove garlic, crushed
¼ cup soy sauce
¼ cup dry sherry
2 cups thinly sliced mushrooms
one 8½-ounce can bamboo
shoots, drained
¼ cup finely chopped green
onion

1. Wipe steak well with damp paper towels. Cut meat into ¾-inch cubes, trimming away and discarding fat.

2. Heat oil in large skillet over medium heat; add steak and garlic and sauté, turning meat to brown all sides lightly.

3. Add soy sauce and sherry. Reduce heat to low and simmer, covered, for 30 minutes. Add mushrooms, drained bamboo shoots and green onion; cook 5 to 10 minutes longer, until mushroom slices are just tender.

Serves 4. Shown on page 65.

Three Country Casserole

2½- to 3-pound chuck steak,
¾ inch thick
2 tablespoons vegetable oil
1 cup chopped onion
1 clove garlic, crushed
1 teaspoon curry powder
one 10¾-ounce can tomato soup
½ cup red wine
one 16-ounce can chow mein
vegetables, rinsed and drained

1. Wipe steak well with damp paper towels. Heat oil in large skillet over medium heat; add steak and sauté quickly to brown, about 2 minutes per side. Remove steak and set aside.

2. Add onion and garlic to drippings in skillet; sauté until tender, about 5 minutes, stirring constantly. Stir in curry and cook 1 minute longer.

3. Add tomato soup and red wine; stir well. Stir in chow mein vegetables. Place steak on top of vegetables. Reduce heat to low and simmer, covered, for 30 to 45 minutes or until meat is tender.

Serves 4.

◎ *MoneySaving Tip:* You can substitute beef broth in recipes calling for sherry or red wine. Buy the canned variety or use bouillon cubes or powdered concentrate, which comes in an envelope. For a tangy flavor, substitute a mixture of half beef broth and half lemon juice for the amount of wine specified in the recipe.

California Beef

2 pounds top round steak
2 tablespoons vegetable oil
1 cup chopped onion
1 clove garlic, crushed
1 cup dry red wine
one 8-ounce can tomato sauce
2 cups thinly sliced mushrooms
1 cup sour cream

1. Wipe steak well with damp paper towels; cut meat into ¾-inch cubes. Heat oil in large skillet over medium heat; add beef cubes a few at a time and sauté for about 5 minutes, turning to brown all sides. Remove beef as browned and set aside.

2. Add onion and garlic to drippings in skillet; sauté until onion is tender, about 5 minutes, stirring constantly. Return meat to skillet. Stir in wine and reduce heat to low; cook, covered, for 30 minutes, stirring frequently.

3. Stir in tomato sauce and mushrooms; simmer, covered, 10 to 15 minutes longer, until meat and mushrooms are tender. Stir in sour cream; heat thoroughly but do not boil. Serve over cooked rice.

Serves 4.

Braised Round Steak

2-pound bottom round steak
instant meat tenderizer
2 tablespoons vegetable oil
2 cups sliced mushrooms
1 cup chopped red onion
one 10½-ounce can clear onion soup
½ cup dry white wine
¼ cup Dijon-style mustard

1. Wipe steak well with damp paper towels. Sprinkle steak with instant meat tenderizer according to label directions; pierce both sides with fork. Cut steak into 4 equal pieces.

2. Heat oil in medium skillet over medium heat; add steaks and sauté quickly to brown, about 2 minutes per side. Place meat in large baking dish or roasting pan. Cover with mushrooms and onion.

3. In small bowl, beat together onion soup, white wine and mustard; pour over steaks. Cover dish tightly with foil. Bake at 350° F for 40 to 45 minutes or until steaks are tender.

Serves 4.

Italian-Style Beef Rolls

1½-pound round steak, ½ inch thick

2 sweet Italian-style sausages

¾ cup chopped onion

1 cup finely diced mozzarella cheese

2 tablespoons grated Parmesan cheese

½ teaspoon basil

1 egg, beaten

1 cup dry red wine

one 6-ounce can tomato paste

1. Using very sharp knife, cut steak horizontally in half, making 2 large pieces each ¼ inch thick. Cut each large piece into 3 equal portions. Place each portion between two sheets of waxed paper; using wooden mallet or rolling pin, pound thin. Set meat aside.

2. Remove meat from sausage casings and crumble meat into medium skillet; brown for 3 to 4 minutes over medium heat. Remove from skillet with slotted spoon and set aside.

3. Pour off and reserve drippings, leaving 2 tablespoons in skillet. Add onion to drippings in skillet; sauté until tender, about 5 minutes.

4. In small bowl, mix sausage meat, onion, mozzarella and Parmesan cheese, basil and beaten egg. Divide stuffing into 6 equal portions; spread 1 portion over each piece of meat. Roll up meat jelly-roll fashion; secure with toothpicks.

5. Return reserved drippings to skillet; add rolls two at a time and sauté over medium heat, turning to brown all sides.

6. Mix wine and tomato paste; pour into 9 x 12 x 2-inch baking dish. Arrange beef rolls in liquid. Cover dish with foil and bake at 350° F for 1½ hours or until meat is tender.

Serves 4 to 6.

 MoneySaving Tip: Bottom round steak, which comes from the rump of the animal and is slightly nearer the shank, is less expensive (and tougher) than top round steak. You can use bottom round instead of top round, but you must extend the cooking time by 25 to 50 percent (for example, in the recipe above you'd bake the beef rolls for about 2 to 2½ hours). Pounding bottom round and other budget cuts of beef with a wooden mallet or a rolling pin breaks down the surface fibers of the meat; this permits tenderizing ingredients like wine and other acidic liquids to penetrate the meat more quickly and thoroughly.

Marinated London Broil

2¼- to 2½-pound London broil, beef shoulder cut
¾ cup olive oil
¼ cup soy sauce
2 cloves garlic, crushed

1. Wipe London broil on both sides with damp paper towels. Pierce meat on both sides with fork.

2. Combine oil, soy sauce and garlic in 13 x 9 x 2-inch baking dish. Place meat in marinade, turning to coat both sides; cover and marinate for at least 2 hours, turning frequently.

3. Preheat broiler.

4. Remove meat from marinade. Broil 6 inches from heat, 8 to 12 minutes per side, brushing frequently with marinade.

Serves 4.

Stuffed Flank Steak

1½- to 2-pound flank steak
¼ pound sliced Genoa-style salami, chopped
¼ pound sliced precooked ham, chopped
½ cup finely diced Muenster cheese
½ cup dry seasoned bread crumbs
¼ cup grated Parmesan cheese
1 egg, beaten
2 tablespoons butter or margarine, softened
1 cup Burgundy or other dry red wine

1. Wipe flank steak well with damp paper towels. Using tip of sharp knife, lightly score one side of steak into diamond shapes. Set aside.

2. In large bowl, combine chopped salami, chopped ham, diced Muenster cheese, bread crumbs and grated Parmesan cheese. Add beaten egg and toss lightly to combine.

3. Place meat scored side down on work surface. Arrange stuffing along one edge of unscored side; roll up jelly-roll fashion and secure seam with toothpicks or tie string around steak at 2-inch intervals.

4. Rub outer surface of steak with softened butter or margarine. Place seam side down in roasting pan; pour wine into pan. Bake at 350° F for 1 hour, basting frequently.

Serves 4.

Curry-Ginger Beef

2½ pounds chuck beef, cut into 1-inch cubes
2 tablespoons curry powder
1½ teaspoons ginger
½ teaspoon chili powder
¼ cup vegetable oil
1 cup chopped onion
2 cloves garlic, crushed
1 cup chopped tart apple
one 10½-ounce can beef broth
3 to 4 tablespoons soy sauce

1. Toss beef cubes in mixture of curry, ginger and chili powder to coat. Heat oil in large saucepan over medium heat; add beef cubes a few at a time and sauté, turning to brown all sides. Remove meat as browned and set aside.

2. Add onion and garlic to drippings in saucepan; sauté until onion is tender, about 5 minutes, stirring constantly. Add apple; sauté 2 minutes longer.

3. Return meat to saucepan; add beef broth and soy sauce. Reduce heat to low and simmer, covered, for 1 to 1½ hours or until meat is tender. Serve over rice.

Serves 4.

Beef and Onion Goulash

¼ cup vegetable or olive oil
6 cups sliced onions
1½ pounds beef stew meat
1 tablespoon mild or hot paprika
1 cup beef broth
one 8-ounce can tomato sauce

1. Heat oil in large saucepan over medium heat; add onions and sauté until golden and tender, about 5 minutes, stirring constantly to separate slices into rings. Remove from pan with slotted spoon and set aside.

2. Cut beef into 1-inch cubes, trimming away and discarding fat; toss meat with paprika. Add beef cubes a few at a time to oil remaining in pan and sauté, turning to brown all sides. Remove beef as browned, then return all meat to pan.

3. Return onions to pan; stir in beef broth and tomato sauce. Reduce heat to low and simmer, covered, for 1½ hours or until meat is tender. Add a little more beef broth if necessary to keep goulash the correct consistency. Serve with buttered noodles, rice or potatoes.

Serves 4.

Budget Beef Burgundy

2 pounds beef stew meat
¼ cup flour
1 teaspoon garlic powder
1 teaspoon dried parsley
1 teaspoon oregano
1 teaspoon basil
¼ cup butter or margarine
6 cups thick-sliced mushrooms
2 cups silverskin onions
2 cups Burgundy wine
one 10½-ounce can beef broth

1. Cut beef into 1-inch cubes, trimming away and discarding fat. In large, clean brown paper or plastic bag, shake meat with flour, garlic powder, parsley, oregano and basil to coat well.

2. Melt butter or margarine in large saucepan or 4-quart Dutch oven over medium heat; add beef cubes a few at a time and sauté, turning to brown all sides. Remove meat as browned and set aside.

3. Add mushrooms and onions to drippings in pan, adding more fat if necessary; sauté until golden. Add wine and beef broth.

4. Return meat to pan; bring to simmering point. Reduce heat to low and simmer, covered, for 2 hours or until meat is tender, adding more beef broth if necessary.

Serves 4.

MoneySaving Tip: Small whole yellow-skinned onions are the most budget-wise substitutes for silverskin onions. Silverskins are small white-skinned onions which are also known as boilers or creamers. They are quite strong in flavor. While not as economical as regular yellow or Bermuda onions, they can be cooked in a variety of ways, and are particularly good when added to stews like Budget Beef Burgundy (above). As the name "creamer" implies, these onions are excellent when served in a cream sauce (try spicing it with nutmeg or cloves). Silverskins can be transformed into another delightful side dish when baked in a cheese sauce—a piquant change from au gratin potatoes.

Beef Stew Vincenza

1½ pounds beef stew meat

2 tablespoons vegetable oil

2 cloves garlic, finely chopped

one 35-ounce can tomato puree

1½ teaspoons salt

1 teaspoon sugar

1 teaspoon oregano

1 teaspoon basil

¼ teaspoon pepper

one 16-ounce package elbow
  macaroni

¼ cup butter or margarine

¼ cup chopped parsley

1. Cut beef into 1-inch cubes, trimming away and discarding fat. Heat oil in large saucepan over medium heat; add garlic and sauté until brown, stirring frequently. Add beef cubes and sauté, turning to brown all sides.

2. Add tomato puree, salt, sugar, oregano, basil and pepper; stir to blend well. Reduce heat to low and simmer, covered, for 1 to 1½ hours or until meat is tender.

3. Just before serving stew, cook elbow macaroni according to label directions. Drain; toss with butter or margarine and chopped parsley. Serve with stew.

Serves 4.

Short Ribs in Barbecue Sauce

3 pounds beef short ribs

½ cup flour

⅓ cup vegetable oil

SAUCE

1 cup chopped onion

one 8-ounce can tomato sauce

½ cup red wine vinegar

3 tablespoons sugar

2 teaspoons chili powder

1 teaspoon Worcestershire
  sauce

¼ teaspoon dry mustard

1. Wipe ribs with damp paper towels. Coat meat well with flour, rubbing into all surfaces.

2. Heat oil in large heavy saucepan over medium heat; add ribs a few at a time and brown on all sides. Remove short ribs as browned and set aside.

3. To make sauce, add onion to drippings in pan and sauté until tender, about 5 minutes. Reduce heat to low and add tomato sauce, vinegar, sugar, chili powder, Worcestershire sauce and dry mustard; stir to blend.

4. Return ribs to saucepan; stir to coat meat well with sauce. Reduce heat to very low and simmer, covered, for 2 hours or until beef is tender. Stir frequently, adding a little beef broth to pan if necessary to prevent sticking.
   Or place ribs in 13 x 9 x 2-inch baking dish; pour sauce over them, cover dish tightly with foil and bake at 325° F for 2 hours. Turn ribs frequently and add more beef broth if necessary.

Serves 4.

Hearty Beef and Barley Soup

4 beef shanks, bones cracked

½ cup flour

1 teaspoon garlic salt

¼ cup vegetable oil

2 cups julienne strips celery

1 cup coarsely chopped
  tomatoes

1 clove garlic, crushed

8 cups water

one 8-ounce can tomato sauce

1 cup dry red wine

¼ cup pearl barley

½ cup chopped parsley

1. Wipe meat well with damp paper towels. Pat all surfaces of roast with mixture of flour and garlic salt to coat well.

2. Heat oil in large heavy saucepan over medium heat; add meat and brown on all sides. Remove meat and set aside.

3. Add celery, tomatoes and garlic to drippings in pan; sauté until garlic is golden, about 5 minutes. Return meat to pan; add water, tomato sauce and red wine. Stir well. Reduce heat to low and simmer, covered, for 1 hour. Stir in barley and simmer, covered, 1 hour longer, stirring occasionally. Remove from heat.

4. To serve, remove meat from soup. Cool meat slightly and cut into bite-size pieces. Return beef to soup; heat the soup for 2 minutes. Sprinkle with chopped parsley.

Serves 4.

Oxtail Soup

2 pounds oxtail pieces

2 tablespoons butter or
  margarine

2 tablespoons vegetable oil

2 cups coarsely chopped celery

1½ cups sliced peeled carrots

1 cup chopped onion

3 cups water

three 10½-ounce cans beef
  broth

one 8-ounce can tomato sauce

1½ teaspoons salt

¼ teaspoon pepper

1. Wipe oxtail pieces with damp paper towels. Heat butter or margarine and oil in large saucepan over medium heat; add oxtail pieces a few at a time and sauté, turning to brown all sides. Remove meat as browned and set aside.

2. Add celery, carrots and onion to drippings in saucepan; sauté over low heat for about 5 minutes, stirring constantly. Return meat to pan.

3. Add water, beef broth and tomato sauce. Simmer, covered, for 2 hours. Cool and chill soup. Remove fat layer which hardens on surface after being chilled.

4. Remove oxtails from soup; cut off meat and discard bones. Puree cooked vegetables and liquid in blender or food processor. Return to saucepan; add meat, salt and pepper. Heat, covered, over low heat until piping hot.

Serves 4 to 6.

Smothered Blue Cheese Burgers

1 pound ground beef
¾ cup crumbled blue cheese
½ cup finely chopped onion
½ cup butter or margarine

TOPPING

3 cups thinly sliced mushrooms
1 cup thin onion rings
½ cup dry red wine or beef broth

1. In medium bowl, blend together ground beef, crumbled cheese and onion. Shape into 4 burgers.

2. Melt ¼ cup of the butter or margarine in medium skillet over low heat; add burgers and sauté, 3 to 7 minutes per side. Remove from skillet and keep warm.

3. To make topping, melt remaining ¼ cup butter or margarine in same skillet over medium heat. Add mushrooms and onion rings and sauté until golden, about 5 minutes, stirring constantly. Reduce heat to low; add wine or broth and simmer, covered, for 2 minutes. Spoon topping over burgers.

Serves 4.

Mexicana Burgers

1 pound ground beef
1 egg, slightly beaten
½ cup finely chopped onion
½ cup dry seasoned bread crumbs
1 teaspoon chili powder
2 tablespoons butter or margarine
one 15½-ounce can red kidney beans, drained
½ cup sour cream
½ cup grated sharp Cheddar cheese
4 hamburger bun halves, toasted

1. In medium bowl, mix ground beef, slightly beaten egg, onion, bread crumbs and chili powder. Shape into 4 burgers.

2. Melt butter or margarine in large skillet over medium heat; add burgers and sauté, 3 to 7 minutes per side.

3. In small bowl, blend drained kidney beans and sour cream. Spoon some on top of each burger. Cover and cook until topping is hot. Sprinkle each with some of cheese. Use wide spatula to lift onto toasted hamburger bun halves.

Serves 4.

Pepper Burgers

1½ pounds ground beef
2 tablespoons black
  peppercorns, crushed
2 tablespoons butter or
  margarine
2 tablespoons vegetable oil
¼ cup sherry
¼ cup cognac

1. Shape ground beef into 4 burgers; pat both sides of each burger with a little crushed pepper to coat.

2. Heat butter or margarine and oil in large skillet over low heat; add burgers and sauté, 3 to 7 minutes per side. Using slotted spatula, lift burgers to heated serving platter; keep warm.

3. Stir sherry and cognac into drippings in skillet; cook over high heat for 1 minute, stirring briskly. Pour over burgers.

Serves 4.

Sloppy Joe Pocket Sandwiches

1 pound ground beef
1 cup chopped onion
one .75-ounce package onion
  soup mix
one 10-ounce can tomato soup
8 small pita pocket breads
1 cup grated Swiss cheese

1. Brown ground beef in large skillet over low heat for 4 to 5 minutes, stirring constantly to break meat into small pieces. Remove from skillet with slotted spoon; set aside.

2. Increase heat to medium; add onion to drippings in skillet and sauté until golden, about 5 minutes. Return meat to skillet; stir in onion soup mix. Reduce heat to low; cook for 2 to 3 minutes, stirring occasionally.

3. Cut slit in top edge of each pita bread; fill each with ½ to ¾ cup meat mixture. Sprinkle grated cheese over filling.

Serves 4.

⊙ *MoneySaving Tip:* Remember that the longer a burger cooks, the smaller it will be! Whether you choose to broil or pan-fry your burgers, cooking times don't vary. A rare burger needs 3 minutes on each side; 5 minutes per side is required for medium burgers; and the well-done burger gets 7 minutes on each side.

Simple Simon Meatballs

1½ pounds ground beef

½ cup dry seasoned bread crumbs

2 tablespoons grated Parmesan cheese

2 tablespoons chopped parsley

1 teaspoon oregano

1 teaspoon basil

½ teaspoon garlic salt

2 tablespoons olive or vegetable oil

one 16-ounce jar spaghetti sauce

1. In large bowl, combine ground beef, bread crumbs, grated cheese, parsley, oregano, basil and garlic salt. Shape mixture into 24 meatballs, each 1½ inches in diameter.

2. Heat oil in large skillet over low heat; add meatballs a few at a time and sauté, turning to brown all sides completely. Remove meatballs as browned and set aside. Drain surplus fat from skillet.

3. Pour spaghetti sauce into skillet. Bring to simmering point over low heat; add meatballs. Simmer, covered, for 20 to 25 minutes.

Serves 4 to 6.

Susan's Swedish Meatballs

1 pound ground beef

½ pound ground veal or pork

1½ teaspoons salt

¼ teaspoon pepper

½ cup butter or margarine

¾ cup finely chopped onion

1½ cups fresh white bread crumbs

1 cup heavy cream

¼ cup dry sherry

¼ cup water

½ cup milk

¼ cup chopped fresh dill or 2 tablespoons dried dill

1. In large bowl, combine ground beef with veal or pork, salt and pepper. Mix thoroughly; set aside.

2. Melt 2 tablespoons of the butter or margarine in large skillet over medium heat; add onion and sauté until tender, about 5 minutes.

3. Add onion to meat mixture along with bread crumbs and ½ cup of the cream; mix thoroughly. Shape mixture into 36 meatballs, each 1 inch in diameter.

4. Melt a little of remaining butter or margarine in same skillet over low heat; add meatballs a few at a time and sauté, turning to brown all sides completely. Add remaining butter or margarine as necessary. Remove meatballs as browned and set aside.

5. Return all meatballs to skillet. Stir in sherry and water. Simmer, covered, for 20 minutes or until meatballs are tender and cooked through.

6. Stir in remaining cream and the milk; heat but do not boil. Sprinkle with dill just before serving.

Serves 4 to 6.

Sweet-Sour Meatballs

1½ pounds ground beef
½ cup dry unseasoned bread
   crumbs
1 tablespoon chopped parsley
½ teaspoon garlic salt
¼ cup butter or margarine
one 12-ounce bottle chili sauce
1 cup grape jelly

1. In large bowl, combine ground beef, bread crumbs, parsley and garlic salt. Shape mixture into 24 meatballs, each about 1½ inches in diameter.

2. Melt butter or margarine in large skillet over low heat; add meatballs a few at a time and sauté, turning to brown all sides completely. Remove meatballs as browned and set aside.

3. Blend chili sauce and grape jelly with drippings in skillet. Cook over low heat until jelly is melted and mixture bubbles.

4. Return meatballs to skillet; simmer, covered, for 20 minutes, turning occasionally to coat meatballs in sauce.

Serves 4.

Herb and Tomato Meat Loaf

1½ pounds ground beef
two 8-ounce cans tomato sauce
1 cup finely chopped celery
1 cup packaged crushed herb
   stuffing mix
¼ cup grated Parmesan cheese
1½ teaspoons oregano
1 teaspoon garlic powder
½ teaspoon basil
2 tablespoons butter or
   margarine

1. In large bowl, blend ground beef with one can tomato sauce, the celery, stuffing mix, grated cheese, oregano, garlic powder and basil.

2. Divide mixture in half; mold each portion into loaf shape and place loaves side by side in lightly greased, shallow baking pan. Pour remaining can of tomato sauce over both; dot loaves with butter or margarine.

3. Bake at 350° F for 45 to 60 minutes, basting from time to time with pan drippings.

Serves 4 to 6.

⊙ *MoneySaving Tip:* Look for on-sale ground meat combinations to use in your next meat loaf; they're often less expensive than 100 percent beef. Beef, pork and veal complement each other nicely in meat loaf, and can be seasoned in the same way as an all-beef meat loaf. Ham and lamb aren't as good in meat loaf combinations—ham is too lean, lamb too fatty.

Stuffed Pinwheel Meat Roll

1½ pounds ground beef

½ cup dry seasoned bread
   crumbs

1 egg, beaten

2 tablespoons butter or
   margarine

2 cups chopped onions

1 cup diced mozzarella cheese

¼ pound sliced Genoa-style
   salami, chopped

one 10¾-ounce can cream of
   mushroom soup

1 cup sour cream

2 tablespoons sherry

1. In large bowl, combine ground beef, bread crumbs and beaten egg; mix well. Set aside.

2. Melt butter or margarine in medium skillet over medium heat; add onions and sauté until golden and tender, about 5 to 8 minutes, stirring constantly. Let cool.

3. Pat meat mixture into 8 x 12-inch rectangle on sheet of lightly greased waxed paper or foil. Spread onions over meat; sprinkle with diced cheese and chopped salami. Roll up meat jelly-roll fashion, starting from one of short edges. Place seam side down in shallow baking pan. Bake at 350° F for 1 to 1½ hours or until meat is cooked but still moist.

4. Meanwhile, combine mushroom soup, sour cream and sherry in small saucepan. Heat thoroughly but do not boil. Serve alongside meat roll.

Serves 4 to 6.

Savory Beef and Cheese Pie

1½ pounds ground beef

one 15½-ounce can cut green
   beans, drained

one 11-ounce can Cheddar
   cheese soup

1 cup instant mashed potatoes

¼ cup grated mild or sharp
   Cheddar cheese

1. Brown ground beef in large skillet over low heat for 4 to 5 minutes, stirring constantly to break meat into small pieces. Drain surplus fat from skillet.

2. Stir drained green beans and cheese soup into meat; mix well. Pour into lightly greased 2-quart casserole.

3. Prepare instant mashed potatoes according to label directions to yield 3 servings. Swirl over top of meat mixture; sprinkle with grated cheese. Bake at 350° F for 30 minutes.

Serves 4.

Skillet Chinese Beef Casserole

2 tablespoons butter or
 margarine
1 cup chopped onion
1 cup julienne strips green
 pepper
1½ pounds ground beef
one 16-ounce can chow mein
 vegetables, rinsed and drained
one 10¾-ounce can cream of
 celery soup
2 tablespoons soy sauce
one 5-ounce can crisp Chinese-
 style noodles

1. Melt butter or margarine in large skillet over medium heat; add onion and green pepper and sauté until onion is brown and pepper is crisp-tender, about 3 to 4 minutes. Remove from skillet with slotted spoon and set aside.

2. Brown ground beef in same skillet over low heat for 4 to 5 minutes, stirring constantly to break meat into small pieces. Drain surplus fat from skillet.

3. Return onion and green pepper to skillet; add chow mein vegetables, celery soup and soy sauce and stir to mix well. Simmer, covered, for 10 minutes, stirring occasionally.

4. Heat Chinese noodles in 300° F oven or in small skillet over very low heat. Serve Chinese beef mixture over hot crisp noodles.

Serves 4 to 6.

Beef and Corn Casserole

1 pound ground beef
½ cup butter or margarine
1 cup salted cracker crumbs
one 8-ounce can cream-style
 corn
1 teaspoon oregano
1 teaspoon basil
6 slices American cheese
1 large tomato, thinly sliced

1. Brown ground beef in large skillet over low heat for 4 to 5 minutes, stirring constantly to break meat into small pieces. Remove meat from skillet with slotted spoon and set aside. Pour drippings from skillet.

2. Melt butter or margarine in same skillet over low heat; stir in cracker crumbs, cream-style corn, oregano and basil.

3. Layer half of meat in bottom of lightly greased 1½-quart casserole; top with half of corn mixture, 3 slices of cheese (trimming to fit) and half of tomato slices. Repeat layers. Bake at 350° F for 30 minutes or until casserole is very hot and bubbling.

Serves 4.

Farm-Style Beef Casserole

1½ pounds ground beef
¼ cup finely chopped onion
½ teaspoon garlic salt
¼ teaspoon pepper
one 16-ounce can stewed
    tomatoes
one 8-ounce can cream-style
    corn
1 cup grated sharp Cheddar
    cheese

1. Brown ground beef and onion in large skillet over low heat for 4 to 5 minutes, stirring constantly. Add garlic salt and pepper; stir to blend well.

2. Stir in stewed tomatoes with fork, breaking tomato flesh into small pieces; stir in cream-style corn and ¾ cup of the grated cheese.

3. Place in lightly greased 1½-quart casserole; sprinkle top with remaining ¼ cup cheese. Bake at 350° F for 30 minutes or until very hot and bubbling.

Serves 4 to 6.

Mexican-Style Skillet Casserole

1⅓ cups quick-cooking rice
1½ pounds ground beef
1½ cups grated mild Cheddar
    or American cheese
one 15½-ounce can kidney
    beans, drained
two 8-ounce cans tomato sauce
1 teaspoon chili powder
½ teaspoon salt

1. In medium saucepan, prepare rice according to label directions to yield 4 servings.

2. Meanwhile, brown ground beef in large skillet over low heat for 4 to 5 minutes, stirring constantly to break meat into small pieces. Drain surplus fat from skillet.

3. Stir prepared rice, 1 cup of the grated cheese, the drained kidney beans, tomato sauce, chili powder and salt into meat. Simmer, covered, for 15 minutes. Sprinkle with remaining grated cheese.

Serves 4 to 6.

🛟 *MoneySaving Tip:* Don't buy a special herb or spice for one-time use; it will probably lie dormant in your spice rack, losing its potency. Instead, know your seasoning substitutes. For garlic salt, use regular salt in the quantity called for and add one small, crushed garlic clove to it. If you're out of chili powder, substitute paprika in the amount specified in the recipe, and add 4 to 5 drops of hot pepper sauce for each teaspoon of paprika used.

Speedy Moussaka

1½ pounds ground beef
1 cup chopped onion
½ cup grated Parmesan cheese
two 8-ounce cans tomato sauce
1 cup sour cream
¼ cup vegetable oil
1 small eggplant, cut into
⅓-inch-thick slices

1. Brown ground beef in large skillet over low heat for 4 to 5 minutes, stirring constantly to break meat into small pieces. Remove from skillet with slotted spoon; place in large bowl.

2. Increase heat to medium. Add onion to drippings in skillet; sauté until golden, about 5 minutes. Remove onion with slotted spoon and add to meat. Blend in grated cheese, tomato sauce and sour cream.

3. Add a little of the oil to same skillet; add eggplant slices a few at a time and sauté over medium heat until golden and tender. Drain on paper towels. Add more oil to skillet as necessary.

4. Cover bottom of lightly greased 8 x 8 x 2-inch baking dish with one-third of eggplant slices; top with half of meat mixture. Add second eggplant layer, remaining meat mixture and a third layer of eggplant. Cover dish lightly with foil; bake at 350° F for 30 minutes or until casserole is hot and bubbling.

Serves 4.

Rice-Kraut Casserole

one 6-ounce package long-grain
  and wild rice mix
2 tablespoons butter or
  margarine
1 pound ground beef
1 cup chopped onion
¼ cup white wine
¼ teaspoon thyme
one 16-ounce can sauerkraut,
  rinsed and drained
1 cup sour cream

1. Cook long-grain and wild rice according to label directions. Meanwhile, melt butter or margarine in large skillet over medium heat; add ground beef and sauté until brown, about 5 minutes, stirring constantly to break meat into small pieces. Remove meat from skillet with slotted spoon and set aside.

2. Drain all but 1 tablespoon drippings from skillet. Add onion to drippings in skillet and sauté until golden, about 5 minutes. Return meat to skillet; blend in wine and thyme.

3. Layer half of meat mixture in bottom of lightly greased 2-quart casserole. Cover with half of sauerkraut and half of rice. Repeat layers; top with sour cream. Bake at 350° F for 30 minutes.

Serves 4.

Beef and Noodles Hungarian

1½ pounds ground beef

2 tablespoons butter or margarine

2 cups thinly sliced mushrooms

¼ cup finely chopped onion or shallots

1 tablespoon cornstarch

1 cube or envelope beef bouillon

1 cup water

1 cup sour cream

1 tablespoon prepared Dijon-style or spicy mustard

one 16-ounce package egg noodles

1. Brown ground beef in large skillet over low heat for 4 to 5 minutes, stirring constantly to break meat into small pieces. Remove meat from skillet with slotted spoon and set aside. Pour drippings from skillet.

2. Melt butter or margarine in same skillet over medium heat; add mushrooms and onion or shallots, and sauté until golden and tender, about 5 minutes, stirring constantly.

3. Remove from heat; add cornstarch and crumbled beef bouillon cube or powder. Slowly blend in water, stirring well to keep mixture smooth.

4. Return to low heat and bring mixture to boiling point, stirring constantly. Add meat to skillet; simmer, covered, for 10 minutes. Blend in sour cream and mustard. Heat thoroughly but do not boil.

5. Meanwhile, cook egg noodles according to label directions; drain. Serve beef mixture over hot noodles.

Serves 4.

Beef and Noodle Skillet Casserole

2 tablespoons vegetable oil

1½ pounds ground beef

1 cup chopped onion

1 clove garlic, crushed

3 cups tomato sauce

half of 8-ounce package thin egg noodles

1 teaspoon basil

1 teaspoon oregano

chopped parsley (optional)

1. Heat oil in large skillet over medium heat; add ground beef and sauté until brown, about 5 minutes, stirring constantly to break meat into small pieces. Remove from skillet with slotted spoon; set aside.

2. Pour all but 2 tablespoons drippings from skillet. Add onion and garlic to drippings in skillet and sauté until golden, about 5 minutes.

3. Return beef to skillet; stir in tomato sauce, noodles, basil and oregano, mixing well. Reduce heat to low and simmer, covered, for 20 minutes or until noodles are tender. Sprinkle with parsley if desired.

Serves 4.

Beef, Rice and Macaroni Italian

2 tablespoons butter or
  margarine
1 cup chopped onion
1 cup chopped green pepper
1 pound ground beef
one 8-ounce package rice-
  macaroni mix
two 8-ounce cans tomato sauce
½ cup water
one 2-ounce jar sliced
  mushrooms
1 teaspoon oregano
2 tablespoons grated Parmesan
  cheese

1. Melt butter or margarine in large skillet over medium heat; add onion and green pepper and sauté until onion is golden and pepper is tender, about 4 to 5 minutes. Remove from skillet with slotted spoon; set aside.

2. Brown ground beef in same skillet over low heat for 4 to 5 minutes, stirring constantly to break meat into small pieces. Stir in rice-macaroni mix and the flavor package included; cook for 2 minutes.

3. Add cooked vegetables to meat mixture; stir in tomato sauce, water, undrained mushrooms and oregano. Simmer, covered, for 15 minutes or until rice is tender; add a little more liquid if necessary. Sprinkle with grated cheese just before serving.

Serves 4.

Saturday Lunch Beef-and-Shells Casserole

2 tablespoons butter or
  margarine
½ cup chopped onion
1½ pounds ground beef
two 15-ounce cans macaroni
  shells in tomato sauce
1 teaspoon basil
1 teaspoon oregano
2 tablespoons grated Parmesan
  cheese

1. Melt butter or margarine in large skillet over medium heat; add onion and sauté until golden and tender, about 5 minutes. Remove from skillet with slotted spoon; set aside.

2. Brown ground beef in same skillet over low heat for 4 to 5 minutes, stirring constantly to break meat into small pieces.

3. Return onion to skillet; stir in macaroni shells in tomato sauce, basil and oregano. Simmer, covered, for 10 to 15 minutes. Sprinkle with grated cheese just before serving.

Serves 4.

Taco Con Carne

2 tablespoons butter or margarine

1½ pounds ground beef

2 cups grated Cheddar cheese

2 tablespoons grated Parmesan cheese

one 5-ounce package taco chips, broken into bite-size pieces

one 8-ounce can tomato sauce

1 teaspoon chili powder

one 1¾-ounce package taco sauce mix

1. Melt butter or margarine in large skillet over medium heat; add ground beef and sauté until brown, about 5 minutes, stirring constantly to break meat into small pieces. Drain off surplus fat.

2. Stir Cheddar and Parmesan cheese, broken taco chips (reserving ½ cup), tomato sauce and chili powder into meat in skillet.

3. Make taco sauce in small saucepan according to label directions, using ½ cup water; stir into meat-cheese mixture.

4. Spoon into lightly greased 2-quart casserole; sprinkle with reserved taco chip pieces. Bake at 350° F for 30 minutes.

Serves 4.

Hamburger Wellington

1½ pounds ground beef

½ cup dry seasoned bread crumbs

1 tablespoon Worcestershire sauce

1 egg, beaten

½ pound liverwurst, at room temperature

one 8-ounce package cream cheese, at room temperature

one 8-ounce package refrigerator crescent rolls

1. In large bowl, combine ground beef, bread crumbs, Worcestershire sauce and beaten egg; mix thoroughly. Mold into loaf shape; place in shallow baking pan. Bake at 350° F for 1 hour. Let cool completely, about 1½ hours.

2. In small bowl, beat together liverwurst and cream cheese until very smooth. Spread over top and sides of meat loaf.

3. Preheat oven to 400° F.

4. Unroll crescent roll dough in shallow baking pan. Pat dough together to seal perforations and gently press into 8 x 12-inch rectangle.

5. Carefully set coated meat loaf in center of dough. Lift sides of dough to cover meat loaf completely, dampening edges to seal. Bake for 15 to 20 minutes; lower oven heat to 325° F and cook 15 minutes longer to heat meat through.

Serves 4 to 6.

Celery-Cream Beef with Almonds

one 5-ounce jar dried beef

2 tablespoons butter or margarine

1 cup chopped onion

2 hard-cooked eggs, coarsely chopped

one 10¾-ounce can cream of celery soup

1 cup water

¼ cup dry sherry

½ cup slivered almonds

1. Separate dried beef into slices; place in small bowl and cover with boiling water. Let stand for 30 seconds; drain and cut beef into bite-size pieces.

2. Melt butter or margarine in large skillet over medium heat; add onion and sauté until tender, about 5 minutes, stirring constantly.

3. Stir in beef, chopped eggs, celery soup, 1 cup water, sherry and almonds. Reduce heat to low and simmer, covered, for 10 minutes. Serve over buttered toast points.

Serves 4.

Stuffed Eggplant

2 medium eggplants

¼ cup olive or vegetable oil

1 clove garlic, split

½ pound ground beef

one 8-ounce can tomato sauce

½ cup cooked rice

2 teaspoons curry powder

½ cup dry seasoned bread crumbs

2 tablespoons butter or margarine

1 cup beef broth

1. Cut each eggplant lengthwise in half and scoop out pulp, leaving shell about ¼ inch thick. Chop eggplant pulp; set aside pulp and shells.

2. Heat oil in large skillet over medium heat; add garlic and sauté until brown, then discard garlic. Add ground beef to skillet; cook until brown, about 3 to 4 minutes, stirring constantly to break meat into small pieces.

3. Reduce heat to low; add eggplant pulp and continue cooking until eggplant is tender, about 10 minutes, stirring constantly. Stir in tomato sauce, rice and curry powder; mix well.

4. Divide mixture among 4 eggplant shells; sprinkle with bread crumbs and dot with butter or margarine. Place in shallow baking dish or roasting pan; pour beef broth around eggplant. Bake at 350° F for 30 minutes, basting occasionally with broth.

Serves 4.

Stuffed Cabbage

1 **small head cabbage**
1 **pound ground beef**
1 **cup finely chopped onion**
½ **cup uncooked long-grain rice**
2 **tablespoons sugar**
1 **egg, beaten**

SAUCE

one **35-ounce can stewed tomatoes**
1 **cup chopped onion**
1 **cup chopped tart apple**
2 **tablespoons sugar**
2 **teaspoons salt**

1. Bring 2 quarts salted water to boiling point in large saucepan. Plunge cabbage into water; turn off heat. Let cabbage stand, covered, for 15 minutes.

2. Meanwhile, combine ground beef, 1 cup finely chopped onion, the rice, sugar and beaten egg in medium bowl; mix thoroughly.

3. Remove cabbage from water. Break off leaves and pat them dry on paper towels. With sharp knife, cut out thick center vein of each leaf, being careful not to cut leaf in half.

4. Place 2 to 3 tablespoons meat mixture at top edge of each leaf. Fold sides of leaf to center; roll up leaf jelly-roll fashion. Secure with toothpicks.

5. To make sauce, combine stewed tomatoes, 1 cup chopped onion, the chopped apple, sugar and salt in large skillet or saucepan. Bring to boiling point.

6. Reduce heat to low and add cabbage rolls in one layer. Simmer, covered, for 1 to 1½ hours or until meat-rice mixture is tender.

Makes about 20 rolls; serves 8.

Note: Divide Stuffed Cabbage between two medium skillets or saucepans to cook if necessary.

MoneySaving Tip: Onions are a year-round budget vegetable that can be put to a multitude of uses. Besides pressing them into service in sauces, salads, casseroles and skillet dishes, you can stuff them with a variety of fillings and serve them as the main course. To substitute onions for cabbage in the above recipe, parboil 1½ pounds large yellow onions until they're just tender—this should take about 15 minutes. Cool them, then remove the onion layers one by one. Chop the center portions and add the chopped onion to the stuffing mixture. Use the larger layers to roll around the filling: lay each onion layer flat, add a tablespoon or so of stuffing, fold the onion up and secure it with a toothpick or two. Then simmer in a robust tomato sauce until the meat filling is cooked.

Corned Beef Casserole

2 tablespoons butter or
  margarine

¾ cup chopped onion

two 12-ounce cans corned beef

one 11-ounce can Cheddar
  cheese soup

½ cup grated sharp Cheddar
  cheese

one 8-ounce package
  refrigerator biscuits

1. Melt butter or margarine in small skillet over medium heat; add onion and sauté until tender, about 3 to 4 minutes, stirring constantly.

2. In large bowl, crumble corned beef with fork; stir in onion. Blend in cheese soup and grated cheese.

3. Pour mixture into lightly greased 8 x 8 x 2-inch baking dish; bake at 450° F for 10 minutes. Top with refrigerator biscuits; bake 8 to 10 minutes longer or until biscuits are golden brown.

Serves 4.

Pork, Ham and Sausage

Pork's adaptability and versatility make it a favorite with many people. Unlike ham, which is salted and smoked, pork is uncured meat. It combines particularly well with tangy flavorings in dishes like Spiced Pork Roast and pungent Glazed Pork Shoulder and Curried Fruit.

Shoulder is the thriftiest cut, both for roasts and chops, but do look for pork loin on sale. Check package labeling to be sure the meat you buy is as fresh as possible, and store pork for no more than two days after cooking. All pork products should be cooked to an internal temperature of 185° F; take care that they are never undercooked.

Ham is a festive meat. Its warm color is beautifully complemented by bright green and yellow vegetables and colorful fruits that let you set a holiday table any day of the year. Unless you have a very large family, a ham roast should be good for two or three extra meals. Try putting the leftovers into tasty, hearty dishes like Ham Croquettes and Savory Ham and Pasta Casserole.

Technically, sausages are ground, seasoned, cured pork meat stuffed into casings. In all of their variations, including frankfurters, kielbasa and knockwurst, they are extremely adaptable and one of the best buys in the meat department. You'll love the variety and ease of dishes like Sausage Alsace Style, Skillet Sausage and Peppers, and Hot Dogs Hawaiian.

So if you have a yen for pork or ham for supper tonight, flip through this chapter before heading for the store. You're sure to find just the right recipe for a great—and inexpensive—main dish.

Pork Roast with Onions and Potatoes

2-pound boneless pork loin roast

1 clove garlic, crushed

¼ teaspoon thyme

4 medium onions, peeled and halved

4 medium potatoes, peeled and halved

2 tablespoons butter or margarine, melted

1 cup dry white wine or chicken broth

1. Rub pork roast very well with garlic and thyme. Place in medium-size roasting pan.

2. Toss onion and potato halves in melted butter or margarine. Surround roast with onions and potatoes; pour wine or chicken broth into pan. Roast at 350° F for 1½ hours; turn onions and potatoes from time to time to brown and cook evenly.

Serves 4.

Pork Roast with Sauerkraut

two 16-ounce cans sauerkraut, rinsed and drained

one 10¾-ounce can chicken broth

1 cup dry white wine

one-half pork loin roast, 6-rib size (2½ to 3 pounds)

2 tablespoons Dijon-style mustard

4 slices bacon

1. Spread sauerkraut over bottom of roasting pan; pour in chicken broth and wine.

2. Wipe pork loin roast well with damp paper towels. Using tip of small knife, lightly score surface into diamond shapes. Rub meat well with mustard.

3. Place roast curved rib side down on sauerkraut. Cover surface of meat with bacon slices. Roast at 350° F for 1½ to 2 hours or until meat thermometer inserted in thickest part of roast reads 170° F.

Serves 4.

Spiced Pork Roast

3- to 5-pound pork shoulder roast

½ cup ketchup

3 tablespoons sherry

2 tablespoons prepared spicy mustard

1 tablespoon soy sauce

1. Place pork roast in large roasting pan; roast at 350° F for 2¼ to 3¾ hours, allowing 45 minutes per pound. Baste frequently with drippings.

2. Meanwhile, blend ketchup, sherry, mustard and soy sauce in small bowl. Brush sauce over roast several times during last 45 minutes of cooking time.

A small roast serves 4; a large roast serves 8.

Glazed Pork Shoulder and Curried Fruit

3½- to 4-pound boneless fresh pork shoulder

one 12-ounce jar apricot preserves

1 cup apricot or fruit brandy

1 tablespoon prepared Dijon-style or mild mustard

one 16-ounce package mixed dried fruits

1½ teaspoons curry powder

1. Wipe pork well with damp paper towels. Place meat in large roasting pan; roast at 350° F for 2½ to 3 hours or until meat thermometer inserted in meat reads 170° F.

2. Meanwhile, mix apricot preserves, brandy and mustard in small saucepan. Stir to blend over low heat; brush glaze on meat several times during last hour of cooking time.

3. In medium saucepan, cook dried fruits according to label directions, adding curry to cooking water. Drain fruit; place around meat 15 minutes before end of roasting time and baste with the apricot-mustard glaze.

Serves 8.

Herbed Pork Shoulder

5- to 6-pound pork shoulder

1 clove garlic, halved

1 teaspoon powdered thyme

1 teaspoon crumbled sage

1 cup dry white wine

8 small onions, peeled

4 medium potatoes, peeled and halved

1. Wipe pork shoulder well with damp paper towels. Rub meat well with cut surfaces of garlic, then rub with thyme and sage.

2. Place pork in large roasting pan; pour wine around meat. Roast at 350° F for 2½ to 3 hours, basting frequently with pan drippings.

3. Meanwhile, place onions and potatoes in large saucepan; cover with salted water. Bring to boiling point; reduce heat to low and simmer, covered, for 15 minutes. Remove vegetables with slotted spoon and pat dry.

4. Add onions and potatoes to roasting pan 30 minutes before end of cooking time, turning to coat them in pan drippings. Cook until vegetables are golden, basting frequently.

Serves 8.

Pork Chops and Caraway Cabbage

4 pork shoulder chops, ¾ inch thick
1 cup chopped onion
1 clove garlic, crushed
4 cups shredded cabbage
2 teaspoons caraway seeds
1½ teaspoons salt
¼ teaspoon pepper
1 cup dry white wine or chicken broth

1. Wipe meat with damp paper towels. Trim a little fat from edge of each chop; melt fat in large skillet over low heat to coat bottom of skillet. Discard trimmings.

2. Increase heat to medium; add pork chops and brown, 4 minutes per side. Remove from skillet; set aside.

3. Add onions and garlic to drippings in skillet; sauté for 5 minutes, stirring constantly. Stir in shredded cabbage, caraway seeds, salt and pepper; sauté 2 minutes longer.

4. Place pork chops on top of cabbage; pour in wine or chicken broth. Reduce heat to low and simmer, covered, for 45 to 50 minutes or until meat is tender.

Serves 4.

Pork Chops Italian Style

¼ cup olive or vegetable oil
1 clove garlic, split
4 pork shoulder chops, ¾ inch thick
one 6-ounce can tomato paste
one 16-ounce can peeled whole tomatoes
1 teaspoon basil
1 teaspoon oregano
1 teaspoon red pepper flakes
2 cups julienne strips green pepper

1. Heat oil in large skillet over medium heat; add garlic and sauté until brown, then discard. In same skillet, brown chops until golden brown, 4 minutes per side. Remove from skillet; set aside.

2. Blend tomato paste into drippings in skillet; cook over low heat for about 3 minutes. Add undrained tomatoes, stirring to break into small pieces. Stir in basil, oregano and red pepper.

3. Mix in green pepper strips. Place chops in sauce; simmer, covered, for 1 hour or until pork is tender.

Serves 4.

Pork Chops Parmigiana

6 pork shoulder chops, ¾ inch thick

1 egg, beaten

½ cup dry seasoned bread crumbs

2 tablespoons olive or vegetable oil

one 8-ounce can tomato sauce

1 cup grated mozzarella cheese

2 tablespoons grated Parmesan cheese

½ teaspoon oregano

½ teaspoon basil

1. Preheat oven to 450° F.

2. Wipe meat with damp paper towels. Dip chops into beaten egg and then into bread crumbs to coat.

3. Pour oil into 13 x 9 x 2-inch baking dish, swirling oil to coat bottom of dish. Place dish in oven for 5 minutes; remove and place chops in dish. Bake for 30 minutes, turning meat after 15 minutes.

4. Remove meat from oven; reduce heat to 350° F. Drain surplus fat from pan. Top each chop with 1 tablespoon tomato sauce and 3 tablespoons grated mozzarella cheese. Pour remaining tomato sauce over chops and sprinkle with mixture of Parmesan cheese, oregano and basil. Bake for 30 minutes or until cheese is melted and tomato sauce is bubbling.

Serves 6.

Pork Chops and Peppers

6 pork shoulder chops, ½ inch thick

3 cups onion rings

4 cups julienne strips green pepper

1½ teaspoons salt

½ teaspoon pepper

1 cup dry white wine

1. Wipe meat with damp paper towels. Trim a little fat from edge of each chop; melt fat in large skillet over low heat to coat bottom of skillet. Discard trimmings.

2. Increase heat to medium; add pork chops and brown, 4 minutes per side. Remove from skillet; set aside.

3. Add onions to drippings in skillet; sauté for 5 minutes, stirring constantly. Add green pepper strips and sauté 5 minutes longer.

4. Return pork chops to skillet, sprinkling with salt and pepper. Pour in wine. Reduce heat to low and simmer, covered, for 40 to 45 minutes or until meat is tender.

Serves 6.

Pork and Rice Casserole

4 pork shoulder chops, ¾ inch
  thick
1 cup uncooked long-grain rice
one 10½-ounce can beef
  bouillon
one 10¾-ounce can onion soup
one 8-ounce can tomato sauce
1 bay leaf

1. Trim a little fat from edge of each pork chop; melt fat in large skillet over low heat to coat bottom of skillet. Discard trimmings.

2. Increase heat to medium and sauté pork chops until golden brown, about 4 minutes per side.

3. Place rice in bottom of shallow 2-quart casserole; stir in beef bouillon, onion soup, tomato sauce and bay leaf. Place chops on top of rice mixture. Cover casserole tightly with lid or heavy-duty foil; bake at 350° F for 1 hour or until meat is tender. Remove bay leaf.

Serves 4.

Sweet-Sour Pork Chops

6 pork shoulder chops, ½ inch
  thick
½ cup sugar
3 tablespoons cornstarch
1 cup beef broth
½ cup red wine vinegar
2 tablespoons soy sauce
one 15-ounce can pineapple
  chunks, drained
1 cup julienne strips green
  pepper
1 cup onion rings

1. Trim a little fat from edge of each pork chop; melt fat in large skillet over low heat to coat bottom of skillet. Discard trimmings.

2. Increase heat to medium; add chops and sauté until golden brown, about 4 minutes per side. Remove from skillet; set aside.

3. In small bowl, blend sugar, cornstarch, beef broth, vinegar and soy sauce. Add to skillet and bring to boiling point over low heat, stirring constantly until mixture thickens.

4. Stir in drained pineapple chunks, green pepper strips and onion rings. Set pork chops on top of pineapple and vegetables; simmer, covered, for 40 to 45 minutes or until pork is tender. Add a little more beef broth if sauce becomes too thick.

Serves 6.

Pork Chops Vino Bianco

4 slices bacon
4 pork shoulder chops, ¾ inch
   thick
1 teaspoon salt
½ teaspoon pepper
4 cups sliced onions
1 cup dry white wine
1 cup chicken broth

1. Fry bacon in large skillet over medium heat until crisp. Drain on paper towels; crumble and set aside.

2. Season both sides of pork chops with salt and pepper; add to fat in skillet and sauté until golden brown, about 5 minutes per side. Remove from skillet and set aside.

3. Add onion slices to drippings in skillet; toss and cook for 2 minutes. Add wine, chicken broth and crumbled bacon. Place pork chops on top of onions. Reduce heat to low and simmer, covered, for 1 hour or until chops are tender.

Serves 4.

Spicy Rib Ends

4 pounds pork loin rib ends
1 cup dry red wine
1 cup red wine vinegar
¼ cup soy sauce
¼ cup honey
1 clove garlic, crushed

1. Wipe ribs with damp paper towels. Place meat in large saucepan and cover with cold water. Bring to boiling point over low heat; simmer, covered, for 3 to 4 minutes. Remove ribs; drain and cool slightly.

2. In large shallow baking pan, combine red wine, vinegar, soy sauce, honey and garlic. Place ribs in mixture, turning to coat well in marinade. Cover and chill for at least 6 hours or overnight; turn ribs frequently.

3. Drain marinade from ribs into small saucepan. Simmer marinade, uncovered, over medium heat until reduced to half. Place ribs in 13 x 9 x 2-inch baking pan; bake at 325° F for 1 hour, basting frequently with hot marinade.

Serves 4.

◎ *MoneySaving Tip:* Be on the lookout for pork rib ends on sale. If you can't find any, substitute spareribs, lamb riblets or beef short ribs. The secret in the Spicy Rib Ends recipe is to marinate the ribs as directed to make them succulent and tender.

Curried Ham Roast

5-pound smoked ham butt

1 teaspoon curry powder

1 cup dry white wine or chicken broth

one 16-ounce can crushed pineapple

½ cup brown sugar, firmly packed

2 tablespoons butter or margarine

1 to 2 teaspoons curry powder

1. Remove rind from ham butt roast; trim away and discard fat to leave a ¼- to ½-inch layer. Using sharp knife, score remaining fat into diamond shapes. Rub roast with 1 teaspoon curry.

2. Place in large roasting pan; pour in wine or broth. Roast at 350° F for 1 hour.

3. Meanwhile, heat crushed pineapple, brown sugar, butter or margarine and 1 to 2 teaspoons curry in small saucepan. Brush glaze over ham butt; roast 1 hour longer.

Serves 8.

Crusty Baked Ham

3-pound canned ham

¼ cup butter or margarine

1 tablespoon prepared spicy or mild mustard

1 tablespoon sherry

¾ cup finely diced Muenster cheese

½ cup dry seasoned bread crumbs

1. Place ham in shallow baking dish; bake at 350° F for 30 minutes.

2. Melt butter or margarine in small saucepan. Blend in mustard and sherry; stir in diced cheese and bread crumbs, mixing well.

3. Pat crumb mixture on top of ham; return ham to oven and bake 30 minutes longer.

Serves 8.

Baked Ham Loaf

2 tablespoons butter or margarine

1 cup chopped onion

two 6¾-ounce cans chunk ham

1 egg, beaten

½ cup dry seasoned bread crumbs

1 cup grated sharp Cheddar cheese

1. Melt butter or margarine in small skillet over medium heat; add onion and sauté until tender, about 5 minutes, stirring constantly.

2. Flake ham chunks into large bowl. Stir in onion. Add beaten egg, bread crumbs and grated cheese; mix well. Place mixture in lightly greased 9 x 5 x 3-inch loaf pan; bake at 350° F for 30 minutes.

Serves 4.

Boiled Ham Shank Dinner

3-pound smoked ham shank
2 cloves garlic
1 bay leaf
4 medium potatoes, peeled and halved
4 carrots, cut into 3-inch pieces
1 small head cabbage, quartered

1. Wipe ham shank well with damp paper towels. Place meat in large saucepan and cover with water; add garlic and bay leaf.

2. Bring to boiling point over medium heat; reduce heat and simmer, covered, for 3 hours. Add potatoes, carrots and cabbage 30 minutes before end of cooking time.

3. To serve, remove meat from cooking liquid; place on warm platter. Drain vegetables and place around meat. Serve with spicy mustard or horseradish.

Serves 4.

Ham Croquettes

2 cups ground precooked ham
1 cup dry seasoned bread crumbs
2 tablespoons pickle relish, drained
½ teaspoon curry powder
2 eggs
2 tablespoons water
vegetable oil

1. In medium bowl, blend ham, ½ cup of the bread crumbs, the drained pickle relish, curry and 1 egg; mix well. Divide mixture into 12 equal portions; shape each portion into 2½-inch-long rolls.

2. Beat remaining egg with the water; pour onto plate. Place remaining ½ cup bread crumbs on second plate. Gently roll croquettes in egg mixture to coat lightly; drain slightly. Roll in bread crumbs to coat completely. Shake gently to remove surplus crumbs; chill croquettes to firm coating.

3. Pour oil into large skillet to depth of 1 inch. Heat until surface of oil ripples and is slightly hazy or thermometer reads 375° F. Fry croquettes 2 to 4 minutes or until golden brown.

Serves 4.

Note: This is an excellent use for leftover ham.

Savory Ham and Pasta Casserole

one 8-ounce package tiny pasta shells

½ cup butter or margarine

¾ cup chopped onion

1 clove garlic, crushed

1 cup finely chopped precooked ham

1 cup dry seasoned bread crumbs

1 cup grated sharp Cheddar cheese

1. Cook pasta shells according to label directions; drain well. Meanwhile, melt ⅓ cup of the butter or margarine in large skillet over medium heat. Add onion and garlic and sauté until tender, about 5 minutes.

2. Stir in chopped ham, bread crumbs and grated cheese. Gently stir in cooked pasta shells.

3. Spoon mixture into lightly greased 2-quart casserole; dot with remaining butter or margarine. Bake at 350° F for 30 minutes or until mixture is hot and bubbling.

Serves 4.

Swiss Cheese and Ham Casserole

one 16-ounce package egg noodles

2 cups finely chopped or coarsely ground precooked ham

one 16-ounce container sour cream

1 cup grated Swiss cheese

2 teaspoons curry powder

1. Cook noodles according to label directions; drain well.

2. In medium bowl, blend ham, sour cream, grated cheese and curry; mix well.

3. Place cooked noodles in lightly greased 2-quart casserole; top with ham-cheese mixture. Bake at 350° F for 30 minutes or until mixture is hot and bubbling.

Serves 4.

Note: This is an excellent use for leftover ham.

MoneySaving Tip: Never throw away the bone after you've finished up a baked ham! It provides the classic flavoring for all lentil, bean and pea soups. Simmer the bone as long as possible; any scraps of meat will fall off, adding taste and substance to the stock. If you're not in the mood for soup, wrap the ham bone in a plastic bag and freeze it (up to 3 months) for later use.

Sausage-Stuffed Acorn Squash

2 large acorn squash
1½ pounds sweet Italian-style sausages
2 tablespoons vegetable oil
1 cup chopped onion
½ cup dry seasoned bread crumbs
½ cup heavy cream
½ teaspoon cinnamon
parsley sprigs
carrot curls

1. Cut squash in half and scoop out seeds; place squash hollow side down in large baking dish. Add ½ inch water; cover dish and bake at 350° F for 1 hour.

2. Meanwhile, remove sausage meat from casings and crumble meat. Heat oil in large skillet over medium heat; add sausage and sauté until brown, about 10 minutes, stirring constantly to break meat into small pieces. Remove sausage meat from skillet with slotted spoon; set aside. Reserve drippings in skillet.

3. Scoop out acorn squash flesh, leaving ¼-inch-thick shells. Chop flesh coarsely; add to drippings in skillet along with onion. Sauté over medium heat until onion is tender, about 5 minutes, stirring mixture occasionally.

4. Add bread crumbs, cream, cinnamon and sausage meat to skillet; mix well. Spoon stuffing into squash shells. Bake for 20 to 30 minutes, until very hot. Garnish with parsley sprigs and carrot curls.

Serves 4. Shown on page 66.

Sausage Alsace Style

1 pound smoke-flavored sausages
1⅓ cups instant mashed potatoes
2 tablespoons olive or vegetable oil
2 tablespoons red wine vinegar
2 tablespoons prepared spicy mustard
½ cup finely chopped onion
½ teaspoon salt
½ teaspoon sugar
¼ teaspoon pepper

1. Place sausages in large saucepan; cover with cold water. Simmer, covered, over low heat for 5 minutes; do not boil. Remove pan from heat but do not drain.

2. Meanwhile, prepare instant mashed potatoes according to label directions to yield 4 servings. Place prepared potatoes in lightly greased, shallow 1- to 1½-quart baking dish.

3. In small bowl, combine oil, vinegar, mustard, onion, salt, sugar and pepper. Set aside.

4. Remove sausages from water; cut almost through in 1-inch diagonal slices. Arrange on top of potatoes. Pour some dressing over each sausage. Bake at 350° F for 20 to 30 minutes or until very hot.

Serves 4.

Baked Beans and Sausages

1 pound sweet Italian-style sausages

½ pound frankfurters

2 tablespoons butter or margarine

1 cup chopped onion

¼ cup ketchup

2 tablespoons brown sugar

1 teaspoon dry mustard

two 16-ounce cans oven-baked beans

1. Preheat broiler.

2. Pierce sausages and frankfurters with fork. Broil 6 inches from heat, frankfurters for 10 minutes, sausages for 15 minutes, turning frequently.

3. Meanwhile, melt butter or margarine in small saucepan over medium heat; add onion and sauté until tender, about 5 minutes. Stir in ketchup, brown sugar and dry mustard.

4. Place baked beans in lightly greased 2-quart casserole; stir in onion-ketchup mixture. Arrange sausages and frankfurters over top of beans. Bake at 350° F for 30 minutes.

Serves 4.

Herb Sausage and Egg Supper

1½ pounds herb-flavored sausages

1 cup chopped onion

one 8-ounce package cream cheese, softened

8 eggs

¼ cup milk

2 tablespoons snipped fresh or frozen chives

4 English muffins, split

¼ cup butter or margarine

1. Prick sausages thoroughly with fork. Sauté sausages in large skillet over medium heat for about 10 minutes, turning to brown all sides. Remove from skillet; set aside and keep warm.

2. Add onion to drippings in skillet; sauté until golden, about 5 minutes, stirring constantly.

3. Using electric mixer at medium speed, beat cream cheese in large bowl until soft and fluffy. Add eggs, one at a time, beating well after each addition; beat in milk. Stir in onion and chives.

4. Pour egg mixture into skillet. Cook over low heat, stirring constantly, until eggs thicken and are moist, shiny and tender.

5. Toast muffins; spread with butter or margarine. Arrange 2 halves on each serving plate. Generously pile egg mixture on muffins; surround with sausages.

Serves 4.

Sausage and Eggplant Casserole

1½ pounds sweet Italian-style
   sausages

¼ cup olive oil

1 medium eggplant, cut into
   ½-inch cubes

one 8-ounce can tomato sauce

1 teaspoon oregano

1 tomato, thinly sliced

⅓ cup grated Parmesan cheese

⅓ cup dry seasoned bread
   crumbs

2 tablespoons butter or
   margarine, melted

1. Preheat broiler.

2. Prick sausages thoroughly with fork. Broil 6 inches from heat for 8 to 10 minutes, turning to brown all sides. Remove from broiler and set aside.

3. In 2-quart casserole, combine oil and eggplant cubes, tossing to mix well. Add tomato sauce and oregano; stir to blend. Arrange tomato slices over eggplant mixture; top with sausages. Bake at 350° F for 30 minutes.

4. Meanwhile, combine grated cheese, bread crumbs and melted butter or margarine in small bowl. Spread over top of casserole; bake 10 minutes longer, until crumbs are crisp.

Serves 4.

Italian Sausage and Onions

1½ pounds hot Italian-style
   sausages

4 cups sliced onions

1 cup beef broth

1 cup dry white wine

1 cup uncooked long-grain rice

½ cup chopped parsley

1. Prick sausages thoroughly with fork. Sauté sausages in large skillet over low heat for 5 to 8 minutes, turning to brown all sides.

2. Add onions, beef broth and white wine; bring to simmering point and cook, covered, for 25 to 30 minutes or until onions are cooked and sausages are tender.

3. Meanwhile, cook rice according to label directions; stir in parsley. Remove sausages and onions from broth; serve over rice.

Serves 4.

Note: If desired, make sauce by blending 1 tablespoon cornstarch with a little cold water and stirring into broth remaining in skillet; bring to boiling point over medium heat, stirring constantly. Pour over sausages and onions.

Skillet Sausage and Peppers

1½ pounds sweet or hot Italian-style sausages

6 cups ½-inch-wide green pepper strips

two 8-ounce cans tomato sauce

1 teaspoon basil

1 teaspoon oregano

1. Prick sausages thoroughly with fork. Sauté sausages in large skillet over low heat until golden brown, about 15 minutes, turning frequently. Remove from skillet and set aside.

2. Pour all but 3 tablespoons drippings from skillet. Add green pepper strips to drippings in skillet and sauté over low heat until tender, about 5 to 8 minutes, stirring constantly. Add tomato sauce, basil and oregano; stir to mix well.

3. Return sausages to skillet; simmer, covered, for 30 minutes. Serve with rice or noodles.

Serves 4.

Savory Stuffed Peppers

4 large green peppers

1 pound sweet Italian-style sausages

1 cup diced mozzarella cheese

½ cup chopped pitted black olives

½ cup dry seasoned bread crumbs

1 teaspoon basil

1 teaspoon oregano

one 8-ounce can tomato sauce

1. Cut ½-inch slice off top of peppers; remove seeds. Cook, covered, in boiling salted water to cover for 10 minutes. Remove from pan and drain very well; set aside.

2. Remove meat from sausage casings and crumble meat into large skillet. Brown over medium heat for about 5 minutes, stirring to break meat into small pieces. Add diced cheese, olives, bread crumbs, basil and oregano; stir to mix well.

3. Blend tomato sauce into stuffing mix; divide among 4 peppers. Place in lightly greased, deep 2-quart casserole. Bake peppers at 350° F for 30 minutes.

Serves 4.

Sausage and Ziti Casserole

1 pound sweet or hot Italian-style sausages

one 8-ounce package ziti or macaroni

1 cup ricotta or small curd cottage cheese

1 cup diced mozzarella cheese

3 cups spaghetti sauce or three 8-ounce cans tomato sauce

2 tablespoons grated Parmesan cheese

1. Prick sausages thoroughly with fork. Sauté sausages in large skillet over low heat until brown and thoroughly cooked, about 30 minutes, turning frequently.

2. Meanwhile, cook ziti or macaroni according to label directions; drain. Toss with ricotta or cottage cheese, mozzarella cheese and 2 cups of the spaghetti sauce or 2 cans of the tomato sauce. Place in lightly greased 2-quart casserole.

3. Place cooked sausages over ziti mixture; spoon remaining sauce over top and sprinkle with Parmesan cheese. Bake at 350° F for 25 to 30 minutes, until very hot and bubbling.

Serves 4.

Porkburger-Apple-Potato Platter

1½ pounds ground pork

½ cup dry seasoned bread crumbs

1 teaspoon salt

½ teaspoon powdered sage

1 egg, beaten

2 tablespoons butter or margarine

2 tablespoons brown sugar

¼ teaspoon cinnamon

4 apples, cored and cut into ½-inch-thick rings

1⅓ cups instant mashed potatoes

½ cup grated sharp Cheddar cheese

paprika

1. In large bowl, combine pork, bread crumbs, salt, sage and beaten egg. Mix well and shape into 4 burgers.

2. Melt butter or margarine in large skillet over medium heat; add porkburgers and fry until brown and thoroughly cooked, about 5 to 6 minutes per side. Remove from skillet; set aside and keep warm.

3. Stir brown sugar and cinnamon into drippings in skillet. Add apple slices a few at a time and sauté until golden and tender, 2 minutes per side.

4. Meanwhile, prepare instant mashed potatoes according to label directions to yield 4 servings. Stir in grated cheese.

5. Arrange porkburgers in row down center of large heated platter. Surround porkburgers with row of apple slices on one side of platter, swirls of potatoes on other side. Garnish potatoes with paprika.

Serves 4. Shown on front cover.

Sausage Burgers Creole Style

2 tablespoons vegetable oil

1 cup finely chopped onion

1½ pounds seasoned bulk sausage meat

½ cup dry seasoned bread crumbs

SAUCE

¾ cup chopped green pepper

¼ cup chopped onion

two 8-ounce cans tomato sauce

1 teaspoon brown sugar

1. Heat oil in large skillet over medium heat; add 1 cup finely chopped onion and sauté until tender, about 4 minutes, stirring constantly. Remove from skillet with slotted spoon; place in bowl. Reserve fat in skillet.

2. Add bulk sausage meat and bread crumbs to onion; mix thoroughly. Shape into 8 burgers; set aside.

3. To make sauce, place 1 tablespoon fat from skillet in medium saucepan; add chopped green pepper and ¼ cup chopped onion and sauté over medium heat, about 5 minutes, stirring constantly. Stir in tomato sauce and brown sugar. Reduce heat to low and simmer, covered, for 10 minutes.

4. Meanwhile, sauté burgers in fat remaining in skillet over medium heat until brown and thoroughly cooked, about 5 minutes per side.

5. Arrange burgers on serving platter. Pour a little sauce over burgers; serve remaining sauce alongside.

Serves 4.

Pepperoni Omelet

2 tablespoons butter or margarine

two 4-ounce pepperoni, cut into ¼-inch slices

1 cup chopped onion

12 eggs

2 tablespoons grated Parmesan cheese

2 tablespoons milk

½ cup diced provolone cheese

1. Melt butter or margarine in large, heavy skillet over low heat; add pepperoni slices and onion and sauté until onion is tender and golden brown, about 5 minutes. Remove pepperoni and onion from skillet with slotted spoon; set aside and keep warm.

2. Beat together eggs, Parmesan cheese and milk. Add to drippings in skillet; add more butter or margarine if necessary. Cook omelet over low heat, stirring with fork until eggs just begin to thicken.

3. Remove from heat when top surface of omelet is still moist and shiny. Shake to loosen omelet in pan. Place pepperoni-onion filling across center of omelet; add provolone cheese. Using wide spatula, fold omelet to cover filling; place on serving platter.

Serves 4.

Savory Frankfurter Casserole

1 pound frankfurters

one 11-ounce can Cheddar cheese soup

one 10¾-ounce can cream of chicken soup

one 5-ounce can Chinese noodles

4 slices bacon

1. Cut frankfurters into ½-inch slices. Combine with cheese soup, chicken soup and Chinese noodles; pour into lightly greased 1½-quart casserole.

2. Fry bacon in small skillet over medium heat until crisp. Crumble and sprinkle on top of casserole. Bake at 350° F for 30 minutes, until hot and bubbling.

Serves 4.

Hot Dogs Hawaiian

one 8-ounce can tomato sauce

1 cup chopped onion

¼ cup brown sugar, firmly packed

2 tablespoons vinegar

½ teaspoon dry mustard

½ teaspoon soy sauce

one 20-ounce can pineapple chunks

1 pound frankfurters, cut into thirds

1 cup uncooked long-grain rice

1. In medium saucepan, blend tomato sauce, onion, brown sugar, vinegar, dry mustard and soy sauce. Simmer, uncovered, over low heat for 5 minutes, stirring occasionally.

2. Add undrained pineapple chunks and frankfurters. Simmer, covered, for 15 minutes.

3. Meanwhile, cook rice according to label directions. Serve frankfurters and sauce over hot rice.

Serves 4.

⊗ *MoneySaving Tip:* A variety of thrifty franks and sausages can go into the dishes in this section. Some are a little more expensive than others, but all represent economy for the budget-conscious cook. Besides regular and all-beef hot dogs, try different "wursts" for a change of pace—knockwurst and bratwurst can be found in practically any meat case. One of the least expensive items now on the market in this culinary category is the new chicken frankfurter, which consists of a ground chicken mixture stuffed into sausage casings. It's just as adaptable as its pork and beef counterparts.

Frank and Kraut Casserole

1 tablespoon vegetable oil

1 cup chopped onion

1 clove garlic, crushed

½ cup ketchup

½ cup water

1 tablespoon brown sugar

1 teaspoon dry mustard

1 teaspoon Worcestershire sauce

one 16-ounce can or package sauerkraut, well drained

1 pound frankfurters

1. Heat oil in large skillet over medium heat; add onion and garlic and sauté until onion is tender, about 5 minutes. Stir in ketchup, water, brown sugar, dry mustard and Worcestershire sauce.

2. Add drained sauerkraut to skillet; toss to combine well. Place mixture in lightly greased 1½-quart casserole. Prick frankfurters with fork and place on top of casserole. Bake at 350° F for 30 to 35 minutes, until franks sizzle and sauerkraut bubbles.

Serves 4.

Hot Dog Mash

⅓ cup butter or margarine

1 cup chopped onion

½ cup chopped green pepper

1 clove garlic, crushed

1 pound frankfurters, cut into bite-size pieces

1⅓ cups instant mashed potatoes

½ cup grated American cheese

¼ cup grated Parmesan cheese

1. Melt butter or margarine in medium skillet over medium heat; add onion, green pepper and garlic and sauté until tender, about 5 minutes.

2. Reduce heat to low and add frankfurters; cook, covered, for 5 minutes, stirring occasionally.

3. Meanwhile, prepare instant mashed potatoes according to label directions to yield 4 servings; stir in ¼ cup of the American cheese and 2 tablespoons of the Parmesan cheese.

4. Place frankfurter-onion mixture in lightly greased 1½-quart casserole; cover with potato mixture. Sprinkle with remaining American and Parmesan cheese. Bake at 350° F for 30 minutes.

Serves 4.

Kielbasa and Hot Potato Salad

1½-pound kielbasa or garlic-
   flavored sausage ring
4 medium potatoes, peeled and
   cut into ½-inch-thick slices
6 slices bacon
1 cup chopped onion
½ cup red wine vinegar
½ cup water
1 teaspoon salt
1 teaspoon sugar

1. Place sausage in large saucepan; cover with cold water. Simmer, covered, over low heat for 6 to 7 minutes; do not boil. Remove pan from heat but do not drain.

2. Meanwhile, cook potatoes in boiling salted water in medium saucepan over medium heat until just tender.

3. Sauté bacon in large skillet over low heat until crisp. Drain on paper towels; crumble and set aside.

4. Add onion to fat in skillet; sauté for 5 minutes. Stir in vinegar, water, salt and sugar. Add potatoes and bacon; toss to blend well.

5. Remove sausage from water; place on top of potato salad. Cover and heat for 3 to 4 minutes.

Serves 4.

Knockwurst in Beer

1½ pounds knockwurst
1 tablespoon vegetable oil
3 cups sliced onions
1 bay leaf
one 12-ounce can beer
1 tablespoon flour
1 tablespoon water

1. Prick sausages thoroughly with fork. Heat oil in large skillet over medium heat; add knockwurst and sauté, turning to brown all sides. Remove from skillet and set aside.

2. Add onions to drippings in skillet; sauté until golden brown, 5 to 7 minutes, stirring constantly. Return meat to skillet; add bay leaf and beer. Reduce heat to low and simmer, covered, for 20 minutes.

3. Place knockwurst on serving platter; keep warm. Blend flour with water; add to skillet. Bring to boiling point, stirring constantly. Pour over knockwurst.

Serves 4.

Open-Face Wurst Sandwiches

one 16-ounce liver sausage roll (Braunschweiger), at room temperature

one 3-ounce package cream cheese, softened

½ cup finely chopped sweet pickles

½ cup finely chopped onion

1 tablespoon prepared spicy mustard

4 large slices sour rye bread with caraway seeds

one 3-ounce can French-fried onion rings

1. Preheat broiler.

2. Using electric mixer at medium speed, beat liver sausage, cream cheese, pickles, onion and mustard in medium bowl until soft and well blended.

3. Divide mixture among rye bread slices; spread to cover evenly and smoothly. Broil 6 inches from heat for 5 minutes.

4. Top each sandwich with French-fried onion rings; broil sandwiches 1 minute longer.

Serves 4.

Savory Scrapple Sandwiches

one 16-ounce package scrapple

4 slices bacon

4 large slices pumpernickel bread

8 thin slices tomato

4 thick slices provolone cheese

1. Cut scrapple into 8 slices and set aside. Fry bacon in large skillet over medium heat until crisp. Drain on paper towels; crumble bacon and set aside.

2. Add scrapple slices to fat in skillet; sauté on both sides until crisp and brown. Place 2 scrapple slices on each slice of pumpernickel bread; sprinkle each with some crumbled bacon.

3. Top each with 2 tomato slices and 1 cheese slice. Broil 6 inches from heat until cheese bubbles and melts.

Serves 4.

◎ *MoneySaving Tip:* Scrapple is a good-to-have-on-hand budget staple. Shaped like a meat loaf, it's a mixture of precooked ground sausage or pork meat and cornmeal. Try scrapple slices as a substitute for your breakfast bacon, ham or sausage—they fry up quickly, so will accommodate the morning rush, and make a great accompaniment to eggs. Scrapple can be stored frozen for up to 3 months.

Scrapple Casserole

one 16-ounce package scrapple

2 tablespoons vegetable oil

1 cup chopped onion

1 clove garlic, crushed

2 cups thinly sliced mushrooms

8 eggs

2 tablespoons milk

2 tablespoons grated Parmesan cheese

one 8-ounce can refrigerator biscuits

1. Cut scrapple into 8 slices. Heat oil in large skillet over medium heat; add scrapple slices and sauté on both sides until crisp and brown. Place scrapple slices over bottom of lightly greased 8 x 8 x 2-inch baking dish in overlapping layers.

2. Add onion and garlic to drippings in skillet; sauté until golden, stirring constantly. Spoon over scrapple. Add mushrooms to skillet and sauté until tender, about 5 minutes; reduce heat to low.

3. Preheat oven to 400° F.

4. In medium bowl, beat eggs, milk and grated cheese. Add to skillet. Cook, stirring constantly, until eggs thicken and are shiny, moist and tender. Spoon mixture over scrapple and onions.

5. Place refrigerator biscuits over top of eggs; bake for 10 minutes, until biscuits are firm and golden brown.

Serves 4.

Veal and Lamb

When planning thrifty meals, one of the most important pitfalls to avoid is monotony. Veal and lamb are two tasty alternative meats to spark up your weekly menu planning. Both are a bit of a luxury, but if you look carefully, you can find less expensive cuts, especially for stews.

Veal is baby beef. The very best veal is extremely pale, with no marbling of fat, and comes from milk-fed calves. Darker, fattier meat is the sign of an older animal and should be avoided.

For rich, juicy stews, like Veal-Mushroom Stew or Veal Stew Paprikash, try to find neck and shank meat. And don't worry about the bones; cracked into smaller pieces, they add flavor and body to the sauce if you choose to add them. The marrow of the shank is not only edible, it's delicious! Breast of veal is a real bargain. Roasted as is or stuffed with herbs or spinach or mushrooms, it makes a marvelous dish. You'll find veal shoulder chops and ground veal versatile as well as economical.

Cooked to pink perfection, lamb is a gourmet's delight. Too many people believe they don't like lamb because they've only had it prepared the old-fashioned way—overcooked until it's dry and tough. You owe it to yourself to try one of the special recipes in this chapter, like Orange Pan-Broiled Lamb Chops or Marinated Lamb Chops and Tomatoes.

For the thriftiest buys, look for lamb chops cut from the shoulder or top of the leg, and stew meat from the shoulder or shank. Because of its distinctive flavor, lamb absorbs stronger seasonings well. It is particularly good with garlic, as in Lamb Shanks Greek Style, or offset with the sweetness of apples and raisins, as in gingery Curried Lamb Stew.

If you're looking for something different for your budget dinner tonight, why not choose veal or lamb?

Crisp-Baked Herb Veal Chops

4 large veal shoulder chops, ½ inch thick

⅓ cup butter or margarine

¼ cup vegetable or olive oil

1 cup dry seasoned bread crumbs

2 tablespoons grated Parmesan cheese

1 tablespoon chopped parsley

2 cloves garlic, crushed

1. Wipe veal chops with damp paper towels. Heat 2 tablespoons of the butter or margarine and 2 tablespoons of the oil in medium skillet over medium heat. Add veal chops and sauté until golden, 4 minutes per side. Place chops in lightly greased, large shallow baking dish.

2. In small bowl, combine bread crumbs, grated cheese, parsley, garlic and remaining 2 tablespoons oil.

3. Spoon some coating on top of each chop, pressing to adhere firmly. Dot each chop with a little of remaining butter or margarine. Bake at 375° F for 30 minutes or until meat is tender and moist and topping is crisp.

Serves 4.

Easy Veal Chops Cordon Bleu

4 veal shoulder chops, ½ inch thick

2 tablespoons dry seasoned bread crumbs

½ cup butter or margarine

4 slices Swiss cheese

4 slices precooked ham

½ cup dry white wine or chicken broth

1. Preheat broiler.

2. Wipe veal chops with damp paper towels; dust both sides with bread crumbs. Broil 6 inches from heat, 5 minutes per side.

3. Arrange chops in shallow baking pan; dot with ¼ cup of the butter or margarine. Cover each chop with cheese slice, then ham slice. Place 1 tablespoon remaining butter or margarine on top of each.

4. Pour wine or chicken broth into pan. Bake at 350° F for 45 minutes, basting frequently.

Serves 4.

ⓧ *MoneySaving Tip:* Make your own seasoned bread crumbs from leftover white bread. Trim off the crusts, cut the bread into cubes and whir them in a blender until fine in texture. Spread the crumbs in a thin layer on a baking sheet and dry in a warm (250° F) oven. For each cup of dried crumbs, add 1 teaspoon each salt and powdered thyme and ¼ teaspoon pepper. Store in an airtight container in a cool dry place.

Stuffed Breast of Veal

3-pound breast of veal
⅓ cup butter or margarine
½ cup chopped onion
½ cup chopped celery
½ cup chopped precooked ham
½ teaspoon thyme
1 cup packaged herb stuffing mix
½ cup warm water
2 slices bacon
1 cup dry white wine or chicken broth

1. Wipe veal with damp paper towels; set aside. To make stuffing, melt butter or margarine in medium skillet over low heat; add onion, celery, ham and thyme and sauté for 3 minutes. Stir in stuffing mix and warm water.

2. Stuff veal pocket; secure flap with toothpicks. Place veal in roasting pan and top with bacon slices. Pour wine or broth around roast. Roast at 350° F for 1½ to 2 hours, basting with pan juices, until meat is tender and juices run clear.

Serves 4.

Spinach-Stuffed Breast of Veal

3- to 4-pound breast of veal
one 10-ounce package frozen creamed spinach
1 cup ricotta or small curd cottage cheese
½ cup dry seasoned bread crumbs
2 teaspoons crumbled rosemary
½ teaspoon garlic powder
1 cup dry white wine or chicken broth
2 tablespoons butter or margarine

1. Wipe meat well with damp paper towels; set aside.

2. Cook frozen creamed spinach according to label directions. Place cooked spinach in medium bowl; add ricotta or cottage cheese, bread crumbs, 1 teaspoon of the rosemary and the garlic powder. Stuff mixture into veal pocket; secure flap with toothpicks.

3. Place meat in roasting pan. Sprinkle with remaining rosemary, add wine or chicken broth and dot with butter or margarine. Roast meat at 350° F for 1½ to 2 hours, basting every 20 minutes with pan juices, until meat is tender and juices run clear.

4. To serve, lift roast veal to heated serving platter. Whisk pan juices and any stuffing in pan until smooth; serve alongside meat as sauce.

Serves 4.

⊙ *MoneySaving Tip:* Breast of veal is a flavorful but little-known bargain cut with almost no fat. Its natural pocket is a ready-made container for money-stretching stuffings. With time, patience and a small sharp knife you can remove the bones and make one thin piece of meat that can be rolled jelly-roll fashion around stuffing. If you opt for this method, increase the cooking time of the recipes given here to 2 hours; a meat thermometer should read 170° F.

Breast of Veal with Mushroom Stuffing

2½- to 3-pound breast of veal, bone cracked

1 teaspoon salt

¼ teaspoon pepper

¼ cup butter or margarine

3 cups finely chopped mushrooms

½ cup dry seasoned bread crumbs

½ cup chopped parsley

¼ cup sour cream

6 slices bacon

SAUCE

2 tablespoons flour

¾ cup dry white wine

¾ cup sour cream

2 teaspoons grated lemon rind

¼ teaspoon pepper

1. Wipe veal with damp paper towels. Season all surfaces of meat with salt and ¼ teaspoon pepper; set aside.

2. Melt butter or margarine in large skillet over medium heat; add mushrooms and sauté until tender, about 3 to 4 minutes. Stir in bread crumbs, parsley and ¼ cup sour cream.

3. Stuff veal pocket with mushroom mixture; secure flap with skewers. Place on rack in large roasting pan. Cover with bacon slices.

4. Roast at 325° F for 1¼ to 1½ hours, basting occasionally with pan drippings, until meat is tender and juices run clear. Remove to serving platter to keep warm.

5. To make sauce, sprinkle flour into drippings in roasting pan; stir well to loosen brown particles. Blend in wine. Bring to boiling point over low heat. Beat in ¾ cup sour cream, the lemon rind and ¼ teaspoon pepper; heat but do not boil. Serve alongside veal.

Serves 4 to 6.

Veal-Mushroom Stew

1 pound veal stew meat (neck and shank), cut into ¾-inch pieces

¼ cup flour

1 teaspoon basil

1 teaspoon dried parsley

1 teaspoon salt

¼ cup butter or margarine

¼ cup olive or vegetable oil

2 large onions, each cut into 6 wedges

2 cups sliced mushrooms

2 cloves garlic, crushed

1 cup dry white wine

1 cup chicken broth

1. Toss veal pieces in mixture of flour, basil, parsley and salt to coat.

2. Heat butter or margarine and oil in large saucepan over medium heat; add veal pieces a few at a time and sauté, turning to brown all sides. Remove meat as browned and set aside.

3. Add onions, mushrooms and garlic to drippings in saucepan. Reduce heat to low; cook, stirring constantly, until onions are transparent. Return meat to pan; add wine and chicken broth. Simmer, covered, for 2 hours or until meat is tender.

Serves 4.

Veal Stew Paprikash

2 to 2½ pounds veal stew meat, cut into 1-inch cubes
2 tablespoons flour
2 tablespoons mild paprika
2 tablespoons vegetable oil
2 tablespoons butter or margarine
1 cup dry vermouth or white wine
1 cup chicken broth
1 cup water
4 potatoes, peeled and quartered
1 cup heavy cream
¼ cup chopped parsley

1. Toss veal cubes with mixture of flour and paprika. Heat oil and butter or margarine in large saucepan over medium heat; add veal cubes a few at a time and sauté for 5 minutes, turning to brown all sides. Remove meat as browned and set aside.

2. Add vermouth or white wine, chicken broth and water to drippings in skillet; stir to blend. Add meat; reduce heat to low and simmer, covered, for 1 hour.

3. Add potatoes to stew; cook, covered, 30 minutes longer. Stir in cream; heat but do not boil. Sprinkle with parsley.

Serves 4 to 6.

Creamy Veal Pies

2 tablespoons butter or margarine
¾ pound ground veal
½ cup fresh bread crumbs
¼ cup chopped parsley
1 teaspoon salt
½ teaspoon marjoram or basil
¼ teaspoon pepper
1 egg, beaten
½ cup sour cream
two 8-ounce packages refrigerator crescent rolls

1. Preheat oven to 375° F.

2. Melt butter or margarine in medium skillet over low heat; add ground veal and sauté for 3 to 4 minutes, stirring constantly to break meat into small pieces. Remove from heat.

3. Stir in bread crumbs, parsley, salt, marjoram or basil and pepper; mix well. Add beaten egg and sour cream.

4. Unroll 1 package crescent roll dough on lightly floured board. Form dough into 4 squares, patting together to seal perforations. Repeat with second package.

5. Divide meat mixture into 8 equal portions; place a portion in one corner of each square. Dampen all edges of each square and fold diagonally in half. Press edges to seal well and enclose filling. Bake for 12 to 15 minutes or until pastry is crisp and golden brown.

Serves 4.

Veal Polpetti

1 pound ground veal
½ pound ground pork
½ cup fresh bread crumbs
2 tablespoons finely chopped
  shallots or onion
1 teaspoon crumbled rosemary
1 cup heavy cream
1 egg, beaten
¼ cup butter or margarine
2 tablespoons vegetable oil
½ cup dry white wine

1. In large bowl, combine veal, pork, bread crumbs, shallots or onion, rosemary, ¼ cup of the cream and the beaten egg; mix well. Shape into 36 meatballs, each 1 inch in diameter.

2. Heat butter or margarine and oil in large skillet over medium heat; add meatballs a few at a time and sauté, turning to brown all sides completely. Remove meatballs as browned and set aside.

3. Add wine to drippings in skillet; bring to simmering point, stirring constantly. Add meatballs; reduce heat to low and simmer, covered, for 10 to 15 minutes.

4. Stir in remaining ¾ cup cream; heat but do not boil. Serve over noodles or rice.

Serves 4.

Lamb Chops English Style

4 lamb shoulder chops, ½ inch
  thick
½ cup cider vinegar
¼ cup finely chopped mint
2 tablespoons sugar
½ pound chicken livers
¼ pound sliced bacon
2 cups small mushrooms
2 large tomatoes, halved
1½ teaspoons salt
¼ teaspoon pepper

1. Wipe lamb chops well with damp paper towels. In shallow glass baking dish, combine vinegar, mint and sugar. Add lamb chops and marinate in refrigerator for at least 4 hours, turning frequently.

2. Wash chicken livers under cold running water; pat dry with paper towels. Snip away and discard fat. Wrap each chicken liver in bacon; secure with toothpicks.

3. Remove lamb from marinade; pat dry. Trim a little fat from edge of each chop. Melt fat in large skillet over medium heat to coat bottom of skillet; add lamb chops and sauté 4 to 8 minutes per side.

4. Meanwhile, sauté bacon-wrapped livers for 2 minutes in second large skillet over medium heat. Add mushrooms; place tomatoes in skillet, cut side down.

5. Reduce heat to low and cook, covered, for 8 to 10 minutes or until chicken livers and vegetables are tender. Remove toothpicks from livers. Serve on large heated serving platter with lamb chops.

Serves 4.

Orange Pan-Broiled Lamb Chops

4 lamb leg chops, ¾ inch thick

2 tablespoons olive or vegetable oil

one 6-ounce can frozen orange juice concentrate

¾ cup water

2 tablespoons soy sauce

1 teaspoon ginger

1 teaspoon garlic powder

½ teaspoon dry mustard

1 large onion, cut into 6 wedges

1 large orange, peeled, sectioned and chopped

1. Wipe lamb chops with damp paper towels. Heat oil in large skillet over medium heat; add lamb chops and sauté until golden brown, about 3 to 4 minutes per side.

2. In small bowl, blend together orange juice concentrate, water, soy sauce, ginger, garlic powder and dry mustard. Pour over meat in skillet.

3. Top meat with onion wedges and chopped orange. Reduce heat to low and simmer, covered, for 30 to 35 minutes or until lamb chops are tender.

Serves 4.

Marinated Lamb Chops and Tomatoes

1 cup vegetable oil

½ cup red wine vinegar

1 clove garlic, crushed

1 teaspoon crumbled rosemary

4 lamb shoulder chops, ½ inch thick

one 1-pint box cherry tomatoes, halved

½ cup chopped parsley

1. In shallow glass baking dish, combine oil, vinegar, garlic and rosemary. Wipe lamb well with damp paper towels; add to marinade, turning to coat well. Cover and refrigerate for at least 2 hours or preferably overnight; turn lamb from time to time.

2. Preheat broiler. Remove chops from marinade; reserve marinade.

3. Broil chops 6 inches from heat, brushing frequently with marinade, 5 to 7 minutes per side.

4. Meanwhile, heat ¼ cup reserved marinade in large skillet over medium heat; add cherry tomato halves and cook until tender, about 5 minutes, stirring constantly. Stir in parsley. Arrange lamb chops on heated serving platter; surround with tomatoes.

Serves 4.

Lamb Stew Home Style

2 pounds lamb shoulder, cut into 1-inch cubes
¼ cup flour
¼ cup olive or vegetable oil
3 onions, cut into wedges
3 tomatoes, cut into wedges
1 cup julienne strips green pepper
1 clove garlic, crushed
1 teaspoon crumbled rosemary
¾ cup beef broth
¾ cup dry red wine
¾ cup water
1 bay leaf

1. Toss lamb cubes with flour to coat. Heat oil in large saucepan over medium heat; add lamb cubes a few at a time and sauté, turning to brown all sides. Remove meat as browned and set aside.

2. Add onions, tomatoes, green pepper strips and garlic to drippings in pan; sauté for 3 to 4 minutes, stirring constantly.

3. Add rosemary, beef broth, wine, water and bay leaf. Return meat to pan. Reduce heat to low and simmer, covered, for 2 hours or until meat is tender.

Serves 4.

Curried Lamb Stew

1½ pounds boneless lamb shoulder
¼ cup flour
2 tablespoons butter or margarine
2 tablespoons vegetable oil
2 cups chopped onions
2 cups chopped peeled apples
¼ cup golden raisins
1 tablespoon curry powder
1 teaspoon ginger
2 cups chicken broth

1. Wipe lamb well with damp paper towels; cut meat into ¾-inch cubes, trimming away and discarding fat. Toss meat in flour to coat.

2. Heat butter or margarine and oil in large saucepan over medium heat; add lamb cubes a few at a time and sauté, turning to brown all sides. Remove meat as browned and set aside.

3. Add onions, apples and raisins to drippings in saucepan; sauté until onions and apples are golden, about 5 minutes, stirring constantly. Stir in curry and ginger; cook 2 minutes longer.

4. Return meat to pan; add chicken broth. Reduce heat to low and simmer, covered, for 1¾ hours or until tender. Serve with rice.

Serves 4.

Lamb Shanks Greek Style

¼ cup vegetable oil

2 cups chopped onions

2 cloves garlic, crushed

2 bay leaves, crumbled

1 teaspoon oregano

¾ cup uncooked long-grain rice

one 32-ounce can peeled whole tomatoes

4 large lamb shanks, bones cracked

one 10-ounce package frozen artichoke hearts

1. Heat oil in 4-quart heatproof casserole or Dutch oven over medium heat; add onions and garlic and sauté until tender, about 5 minutes. Stir in bay leaves, oregano and rice.

2. Gradually blend in undrained tomatoes, stirring to break them into pieces. Bring mixture to simmering point; add lamb shanks.

3. Cover casserole tightly and bake at 350° F for 1½ to 2 hours or until lamb shanks are tender. Stir in artichoke hearts 30 minutes before end of cooking time.

Serves 4. Shown on page 67.

Skillet Steak Sauté (*page 11*)

Sausage-Stuffed Acorn Squash (*page 44*)

Lamb Shanks Greek Style (*page 64*)

Calves' Liver au Poivre (*page 77*)

Peachy Roast Chicken (*page 86*)

69

Iced Marinated Mussels (*page 107*)

Three-Cheese Spinach Noodles (*page 117*)

Ratatouille Omelet (*page 124*)

Variety Meats

Any European shopping in an American market is surprised at the low cost of our variety meats. Brains, tripe and tongue, liver, kidneys and sweetbreads are all considered choice treats in so many countries that we Americans should become better acquainted with these tasty meats—especially since they are such good buys.

Calves' liver is the caviar of variety meats—but it's still a bargain when you consider that it contains no bone or fat. Beef liver is lower in price than calves' liver; the frozen prepackaged slices are particularly economical. For a real change, try Calves' Liver au Poivre or Mustardy Baked Liver. Chicken livers, so easy and quick to prepare, can serve as a delicious entrée at any meal. All liver should be as fresh as possible and free of any fat or membrane. It should be cooked so that the outside is crisp and brown while the inside remains moist, with a trace of pink.

Of beef, veal and lamb, veal kidneys are the mildest. Be sure any kidneys you buy are very fresh with no strong ammonia smell. Experiment with succulent Kidney-Mushroom Stew or Kidneys and Onions in Wine.

Tripe is the delicate whitish inner lining of the stomach. Honeycomb is the best type. All tripe is precooked, but it requires soaking and simmering for at least an hour. If you're feeling adventurous, Tripe Marinara is an easy standby, and Tripe Milanese, a spicy classic.

Tongue is one of the most popular variety meats. Lean and boneless, it slices beautifully and can provide two or three days of good eating. For the main course, choose Tongue with Raisin Sour Sauce or Tongue with Wine Sauce. Chilled leftovers taste great in sandwiches and salads.

Brains are white, tender and delicately flavored. If you've never tried them, you might want to introduce them to your family in Brains Beurre Noir, brains served with a nutty flavored butter sauce. Just make sure that they are absolutely fresh and use them within 24 hours of purchase.

For a delightful change of pace that's easy on your pocketbook, add some variety meats to your shopping list and fix some of the delectable dishes you'll find in this chapter.

Liver Cutlets

4 large slices beef liver (about 1 pound)
1 cup dry unseasoned bread crumbs
1 teaspoon oregano
1 teaspoon basil
1 teaspoon garlic powder
1 egg
1 tablespoon water
1 clove garlic, crushed
¼ cup butter or margarine
2 tablespoons vegetable oil
lemon wedges

1. Wipe liver well with damp paper towels; trim off and discard skin at edge of each liver slice. Set liver aside.

2. Combine bread crumbs, oregano, basil and garlic powder; place on platter. Combine egg, water and garlic; pour onto second platter.

3. Dip each liver slice in egg mixture to coat both sides; drain slightly. Dip both sides in bread crumbs; press to coat firmly and gently shake off surplus crumbs.

4. Heat butter or margarine and oil in large skillet over medium heat; add liver slices and sauté 2½ minutes per side for liver to be cooked through but still tender and pink. Serve with lemon wedges.

Serves 4.

Liver Italian Style

6 slices beef or calves' liver (1½ pounds)
½ cup flour
½ teaspoon salt
¼ teaspoon pepper
¼ cup butter or margarine
¼ cup olive oil
6 cups onion rings
2 cups thinly sliced mushrooms
1 teaspoon oregano

1. Wipe liver well with damp paper towels; trim off and discard skin at edge of each liver slice. Mix flour, salt and pepper; place on large plate. Dip both sides of each slice into mixture to coat; set aside.

2. Heat 2 tablespoons each of the butter or margarine and oil in large skillet over low heat; add onion rings, mushrooms and oregano and sauté for 2 minutes. Cover and cook over very low heat until vegetables are tender, about 8 minutes.

3. Meanwhile, heat remaining butter or margarine and oil in second skillet over medium heat. Add liver slices two at a time and sauté to brown, keeping center moist and juicy, about 3 minutes per side for beef liver and 2 minutes per side for calves' liver.

4. Place cooked liver on heated serving platter. Smother with onion-mushroom mixture.

Serves 4 to 6.

Mustardy Baked Liver

4 to 6 slices beef liver (about
  1 pound)

1 egg

1 tablespoon water

½ cup dry seasoned bread
  crumbs

2 tablespoons butter or
  margarine

2 tablespoons vegetable oil

⅓ cup prepared Dijon-style or
  mild mustard

¼ cup dry seasoned bread
  crumbs

2 tablespoons finely chopped
  onion

½ teaspoon basil

½ teaspoon tarragon

½ cup dry white wine or
  chicken broth

1. Wipe liver well with damp paper towels; trim off and discard skin at edge of each liver slice. Set liver aside.

2. Beat together egg and water; pour onto plate. Place ½ cup bread crumbs on second plate. Dip each liver slice in egg mixture to coat both sides; drain slightly. Dip both sides in bread crumbs; pat crumbs firmly to coat.

3. Heat butter or margarine and oil in large skillet over medium heat; add liver slices and sauté to brown and seal coating, 1 minute per side. Place liver slices in single layer in a lightly greased, large shallow roasting pan. Add mustard, ¼ cup bread crumbs, onion, basil and tarragon to drippings in skillet; stir to mix well. Spread mixture over liver slices. Pour wine or broth into baking pan; bake at 350° F for 15 minutes.

Serves 4.

Sherried Calves' Liver

6 slices calves' liver
  (1½ pounds)

½ cup flour

½ teaspoon garlic salt

¼ cup butter or margarine

¼ cup vegetable oil

½ cup dry sherry

¼ cup chopped parsley

lemon wedges

1. Wipe calves' liver well with damp paper towels; trim off and discard skin at edge of each liver slice. Mix together flour and garlic salt; place on large plate. Dip both sides of each slice into mixture to coat.

2. Heat butter or margarine and oil in large skillet over medium heat; add liver slices two at a time and sauté to brown, keeping center moist and juicy, about 2 minutes per side. Do not overcook. Place cooked liver on heated serving platter; keep warm.

3. Add sherry to skillet; heat, stirring constantly to loosen pan drippings. Stir in parsley; pour over liver. Serve with lemon wedges.

Serves 4 to 6.

Calves' Liver au Poivre

6 slices calves' liver
  (1½ pounds)
¼ cup Dijon-style mustard
2 tablespoons black
  peppercorns, coarsely crushed
¼ cup butter or margarine
¼ cup vegetable oil
¼ cup dry red wine
2 tablespoons chopped parsley

1. Wipe calves' liver well with damp paper towels; trim off and discard skin at edge of each liver slice. Lightly spread both sides of each liver slice with a little mustard. Sprinkle both sides with some black pepper, pressing firmly to adhere. Place liver on cookie sheet and chill for at least 30 minutes to firm coating.

2. Heat butter or margarine and oil in large skillet over medium heat; add liver slices two at a time and sauté to brown, keeping center moist and juicy, about 2 minutes per side. Do not overcook. Place cooked liver on heated serving platter; keep warm.

3. Add wine to drippings in skillet; heat, stirring constantly to loosen brown particles. Pour over liver; sprinkle with parsley.

Serves 4 to 6. Shown on page 68.

Chicken Liver Omelet

¾ pound chicken livers
¼ cup butter or margarine
1 cup chopped onion
¼ cup chopped parsley
½ teaspoon salt
¼ teaspoon pepper
8 eggs
¼ cup heavy cream
1 teaspoon salt
3 to 4 drops hot pepper sauce

1. Wash chicken livers well under cold running water; pat dry with paper towels. Using scissors, snip off and discard surplus fat. Snip livers in half and set aside.

2. Melt 2 tablespoons of the butter or margarine in large skillet over medium heat; add onion and sauté until tender, about 4 minutes. Add chicken livers, parsley, salt and pepper. Cook, stirring constantly, until chicken livers are brown but still tender and moist, about 3 to 4 minutes. Keep warm.

3. In medium bowl, beat together eggs, cream, salt and hot pepper sauce. Melt remaining 2 tablespoons butter or margarine in large skillet or omelet pan over medium heat. Pour in egg mixture.

4. Reduce heat to low and cook, stirring constantly, until eggs are slightly thickened. Continue to cook without stirring until underside is golden and top surface is shiny and moist.

5. Arrange chicken liver filling on the third of omelet nearest handle of pan. Using broad spatula, fold omelet into thirds, rolling to far edge of pan. Place on warm serving platter.

Serves 4.

Piquant Liver and Chestnuts

2 pounds chicken livers
½ pound sliced bacon
¾ cup grape jelly
¾ cup chili sauce
⅓ cup soy sauce
two 7-ounce cans water chestnuts, drained and thinly sliced

1. Wash chicken livers well under cold running water; pat dry with paper towels. Using scissors, snip off and discard surplus fat. Snip livers in half and set aside.

2. Sauté bacon in large skillet over low heat until crisp, pouring off fat into liquid measure as it accumulates. Drain bacon on paper towels; break into 1-inch pieces.

3. Return 3 tablespoons bacon fat to skillet; add chicken livers and sauté over medium heat until cooked through but still moist and tender, about 5 to 8 minutes. Remove from skillet with slotted spoon and set aside.

4. Blend grape jelly, chili sauce and soy sauce into drippings in skillet. Bring to simmering point over low heat; add chicken livers and water chestnuts and cook for 2 to 3 minutes. Stir in bacon pieces; cook 1 minute longer. Serve over rice.

Serves 4.

Tongue with Wine Sauce

3-pound beef tongue

WINE SAUCE

3 tablespoons butter or margarine
1½ cups chopped onions
one 10½-ounce can beef broth
1 cup tongue broth
½ cup dry white wine
2 tablespoons cornstarch
½ teaspoon powdered thyme

1. Wash tongue well under cold running water, scrubbing with clean vegetable brush. Trim off and discard fat at root end. Place tongue in large saucepan and cover with water. Bring to boiling point over medium heat. Reduce heat to low and simmer, covered, for 3 to 4 hours or until tender.

2. Remove cooked tongue from pan and cool for 10 minutes. Remove and discard skin; keep tongue warm. Reserve 1 cup tongue broth, skimming off any fat.

3. To make wine sauce, melt butter or margarine in medium saucepan over medium heat; add onions and sauté until tender, about 5 minutes, stirring constantly. Stir in beef and tongue broth.

4. In small bowl, blend together wine, cornstarch and thyme. Blend into mixture in saucepan. Bring to boiling point over medium heat, stirring constantly until thickened. Serve alongside tongue.

Serves 8.

Tongue with Raisin Sour Sauce

2½- to 3-pound smoked beef
  tongue
2 stalks celery
2 carrots
2 onions
6 peppercorns
1 bay leaf

   SAUCE

¼ cup butter or margarine
¼ cup flour
2 cups tongue broth
½ cup golden raisins
¼ cup lemon juice
2 tablespoons sugar
½ teaspoon ginger
½ teaspoon grated lemon rind

1. Wash tongue under cold running water, scrubbing with clean vegetable brush. Trim off and discard surplus fat at root end.

2. Place tongue in 8-quart saucepan along with celery, carrots, onions, peppercorns and bay leaf. Add water to cover. Bring to boiling point over medium heat; reduce heat to low and simmer, covered, for 2½ to 3 hours or until tongue is tender.

3. Remove tongue from pan; place on board and cool for 10 minutes. Reserve 2 cups tongue broth; skimming off any fat. Remove and discard skin from tongue; carve tongue into ¼-inch-thick slices and place on heated serving platter to keep warm.

4. To make sauce, melt butter or margarine in medium saucepan over medium heat. Stir in flour and cook, stirring constantly, until mixture bubbles. Remove from heat; slowly blend in reserved tongue broth, stirring to keep mixture smooth.

5. Return mixture to heat; bring to boiling point, stirring constantly. Add raisins. Reduce heat to low and simmer, covered, for 10 minutes. Stir in lemon juice, sugar, ginger and lemon rind; simmer 5 minutes longer. Pour a little over tongue and serve remaining sauce alongside.

Serves 8.

   MoneySaving Tip: Like other meats in this category, tongue represents economy because it contains very little fat. It also represents variety because it is amenable to so many different sauces and spices, as shown by the three recipes here. It's delicious when served with a robust barbecue sauce too. If you have a pressure cooker, you might prefer to cook tongue in it rather than in a conventional pot—this can save on your energy bills as well as saving on preparation time. After scrubbing the tongue and trimming off and discarding the fat, place the tongue in a large pressure cooker along with 2 cups water. Tightly secure the lid and increase the pressure, following the manufacturer's instructions. Cook the tongue at 15 pounds pressure for 1 hour or until tender. Cool as directed by the manufacturer before removing the lid, then proceed with the rest of the recipe.

Tongue with Mustard Sauce

3-pound beef tongue

2 stalks celery, cut into 1-inch pieces

2 carrots, peeled and cut into 1-inch pieces

2 cloves garlic, cut into slivers

6 peppercorns

1 bay leaf

SAUCE

¼ cup butter or margarine

3 tablespoons flour

2 cups tongue broth

2 tablespoons prepared spicy mustard

1 tablespoon red wine vinegar

1. Wash tongue under cold running water, scrubbing with clean vegetable brush. Trim off and discard surplus fat at root end. Place tongue in large saucepan and cover with cold water; add celery, carrots, garlic, peppercorns and bay leaf. Bring to boiling point over medium heat. Reduce heat to low and simmer, covered, for 3 hours or until tongue is tender.

2. Remove tongue from pan and cool for 10 minutes. Remove and discard skin; keep tongue warm. Reserve 2 cups tongue broth, skimming off any fat.

3. To make sauce, melt butter or margarine in medium saucepan over medium heat; stir in flour and cook for 2 minutes or until golden and bubbly. Remove from heat; slowly blend in reserved tongue broth, stirring to keep sauce smooth.

4. Return sauce to heat. Bring to boiling point, stirring constantly until sauce is thick. Stir in mustard and vinegar. Serve sauce with sliced tongue.

Serves 4.

Kidney-Mushroom Stew

2 beef kidneys

¼ cup red wine vinegar

¼ cup flour

2 tablespoons vegetable oil

2 tablespoons butter or margarine

2 cups chopped onions

2 cloves garlic, crushed

1 cup sliced mushrooms

½ teaspoon powdered thyme

1 cup dry red wine

1 cup beef broth

1. Place kidneys in large bowl with vinegar; add water to cover, and soak for 2 hours. Remove kidneys from liquid and place in saucepan. Cover with water and bring to boiling point. Drain off water immediately; cover kidneys with cold water to cool, then drain.

2. Remove and discard outer membrane from kidneys. Thinly slice kidneys and toss in flour to coat. Heat oil and butter or margarine in medium saucepan over medium heat; add kidneys and sauté for about 2 minutes, turning to brown all sides. Remove kidneys from pan and set aside.

3. Add onions, garlic and mushrooms to drippings in pan; sauté for 5 minutes. Return kidneys to pan; add thyme, wine and beef broth. Reduce heat to low and simmer, covered, for 30 minutes, stirring occasionally. Serve over cooked rice or noodles.

Serves 4.

Kidneys and Onions in Wine

6 veal or lamb kidneys
¼ cup red wine vinegar
¼ cup butter or margarine
8 cups onion rings
1 cup dry white wine
¼ cup chopped parsley
¾ teaspoon salt
¼ teaspoon pepper

1. Peel off and discard outer membrane of each kidney. Using sharp scissors, cut out and discard core from center of inner curve of each kidney. Place kidneys in medium bowl with vinegar; add water to cover, and soak for at least 1 hour.

2. Remove kidneys from liquid; cut lengthwise in half. Place in medium saucepan. Cover with cold water and bring to boiling point; remove kidneys and immediately place in cold water. Set aside.

3. Melt butter or margarine in large skillet over low heat; add onions and sauté for 2 minutes. Reduce heat to very low and cook, covered, until tender, about 8 minutes.

4. Thinly slice kidneys; add to onions along with wine, parsley, salt and pepper. Simmer, covered, until kidneys are cooked but still tender, about 5 to 7 minutes.

Serves 4.

Brains Beurre Noir

3 calves' brains (2 to 2½ pounds)
1 tablespoon salt
1 tablespoon white vinegar
one 10½-ounce can beef consommé
¼ cup red wine vinegar
2 stalks celery
2 small bay leaves
1 small onion, quartered
½ cup butter or margarine
one 3-ounce jar capers, drained

1. Wash brains under cold running water. Place in large bowl; sprinkle with salt and white vinegar. Cover with cold water and soak for 2 hours. Pour off liquid.

2. In large skillet, combine consommé, red wine vinegar, celery, bay leaves and onion. Bring to simmering point over low heat. Add brains to skillet and simmer, covered, for 30 minutes. Baste brains with liquid from time to time.

3. Remove brains from skillet with slotted spoon and place on hot serving platter. Slice thinly; keep warm.

4. Heat butter or margarine and drained capers in medium skillet over medium-high heat until butter browns. Pour mixture over brains. Serve immediately.

Serves 4.

Tripe Marinara

2 pounds precooked
  honeycomb tripe

6 cups cold water

½ cup vinegar

2 cups sliced onions

1 teaspoon salt

one 15-ounce jar spaghetti
  sauce

1. Wash tripe very well under cold running water; cut into 3 x ¾-inch strips. Place in large bowl; cover with 4 cups of the cold water and the vinegar; soak for 1 hour.

2. Remove tripe from bowl and rinse under cold running water. In large saucepan, combine tripe, onions, salt and remaining 2 cups water. Bring to boiling point over medium heat. Reduce heat to low and simmer, covered, for 45 minutes.

3. Pour off cooking liquid. Add spaghetti sauce to tripe in saucepan; simmer, covered, for 15 minutes. Serve with rice.

Serves 4.

Tripe Milanese

2 pounds precooked
  honeycomb tripe

6 cups cold water

½ cup vinegar

4 slices bacon, diced

¼ cup olive oil

2 tablespoons butter or
  margarine

1½ cups chopped onions

¾ cup chopped celery

2 cloves garlic, crushed

1 teaspoon red pepper flakes

2 cups chicken broth

1 cup dry white wine

1 cup uncooked long-grain rice

½ cup chopped parsley

1. Wash tripe very well under cold running water; cut into 1½ x ¾-inch strips. Place in large bowl; cover with 4 cups of the cold water and the vinegar; soak for 1 hour.

2. Remove tripe from bowl and rinse under cold running water. Place in large saucepan with remaining 2 cups water; bring to boiling point over medium heat. Reduce heat to low and simmer, covered, for 45 minutes. Remove tripe and set aside; pour off cooking liquid.

3. Fry bacon in same saucepan over medium heat until crisp; remove from pan with slotted spoon and set aside. Add oil and butter or margarine to bacon fat in pan; add onions, celery and garlic and sauté until onions and celery are tender, about 8 minutes, stirring constantly to avoid burning.

4. Return tripe to pan; add red pepper flakes, chicken broth and wine. Reduce heat to low and simmer, covered, for 30 minutes. Add rice; stir well. Simmer 30 minutes longer, until rice is tender. Stir in chopped parsley.

Serves 4.

Poultry and Seafood

When it comes to thrifty main meals, chicken rules the roost. Rich in protein and low in fat, its tastiness is matched by its economy and versatility. Peachy Roast Chicken, Skillet Chicken and Tarragon Rice, Chicken Rolls Cordon Bleu—this chapter is packed with exciting recipes you and your family will never tire of.

Look for a plump bird that has unbroken skin padded with a fine layer of fat. Cook it within a couple of days of purchase, and store leftovers no longer than two days. Chicken freezes well and, with giblets removed, will keep for six months.

Turkey, too, is a real money saver. Because of increased consumer demand, most supermarkets now stock turkeys all year round. Particularly economical are frozen parts and boneless turkey rolls. Legs, wings and breasts are a good bet for small families who might find a whole roast means too many leftovers.

Both chicken and turkey should be kept moist during cooking to retain delicate flavor and tenderness; avoid overcooking poultry.

Seafood is a different kettle of fish. Even though prices for fish have risen in recent years, it is really a thrifty purchase since there is little or no waste and the protein content is very high. When purchasing fresh fillets, look for clean-smelling, creamy white, moist flesh. Whole fish should have bright bulging eyes, red gills and firm scales. Frozen fish should be in packages that are free of ice crystals and stored frozen until just before use.

Canned fish remains a fine money saver; you'll find some great tuna variations here, including Tuna-Cheese Quiche, Crispy Tuna Hot Pot and Tuna Tetrazzini.

For those with an adventurous palate, a few unusual and delicious but economical seafood specialties have been added, like Squid Salad Vinaigrette and Iced Marinated Mussels, both ideal for parties and buffets.

Whether you want poulty or seafood for dinner tonight, the dollar-stretching recipes here will fill the bill—deliciously!

Lemon Roast Chicken

4- to 5-pound roasting chicken
2 teaspoons salt
½ teaspoon pepper
1 lemon, cut into wedges
4 potatoes, peeled and halved
3 tablespoons vegetable oil
3 tablespoons butter or
    margarine
3 tablespoons lemon juice
1 clove garlic, crushed

1. Wash chicken under cold running water; pat dry inside and out with paper towels. Sprinkle body cavity with salt and pepper. Secure neck skin to back of chicken with skewer; fold wings under. Place lemon wedges in body cavity; secure vent and truss legs in position.

2. Place chicken in roasting pan and arrange potatoes around chicken. Roast at 350° F for 2 hours or until meat thermometer inserted in thigh of chicken registers 180° F.

3. Meanwhile, combine oil, butter or margarine, lemon juice and garlic in small saucepan. Heat over low heat for 2 minutes. Pour over chicken 30 minutes before end of cooking time; baste several times.

Serves 8.

Roast Chicken with Orange Rice Stuffing

3-pound broiler-fryer chicken
⅓ cup uncooked long-grain rice
¾ cup butter or margarine
¾ cup chopped onion
¼ cup coarsely chopped
    walnuts
1 orange, peeled, sectioned and
    chopped
¼ teaspoon thyme
½ cup orange juice

1. Wash chicken under cold running water; pat dry inside and out with paper towels. Set aside. Cook rice according to label directions.

2. Meanwhile, melt ½ cup of the butter or margarine in large skillet over medium heat. Add onion and sauté until tender, about 5 minutes. Add walnuts; sauté 2 minutes longer. Add orange, thyme and hot cooked rice to skillet; toss to mix well.

3. Stuff chicken with rice mixture. Secure neck skin to back of chicken with skewer; fold wings under, secure vent and truss legs in position. Place in roasting pan; rub with remaining butter or margarine. Pour orange juice around chicken. Roast at 350° F for 1¼ to 1½ hours or until tender, basting frequently. Add more orange juice to pan if necessary.

Serves 4.

Herb Roasted Chicken

3-pound broiler-fryer chicken

1 stalk celery, cut into 1-inch
   pieces

1 medium onion

4 whole cloves

2 tablespoons butter or
   margarine, softened

1 teaspoon crumbled tarragon

½ cup dry white wine

1 cup seedless green grape
   halves

1. Wash chicken well under cold running water; pat dry inside and out with paper towels. Secure neck skin to back of chicken with skewer; fold wings under. Stuff body cavity with celery and onion studded with whole cloves; secure vent and truss legs in position.

2. Blend butter or margarine and tarragon; rub onto skin of chicken. Place chicken in roasting pan; pour wine over chicken. Roast chicken at 350° F for 1½ hours or until tender; baste frequently. Add grapes; bake 10 minutes longer.

Serves 4.

Peachy Roast Chicken

3-pound broiler-fryer chicken

1½ teaspoons salt

½ teaspoon pepper

1 small bunch parsley

one 16-ounce can cling peach
   halves

1 tablespoon lemon juice

1 tablespoon soy sauce

chicory leaves (optional)

1. Wash chicken well under cold running water; pat dry inside and out with paper towels. Sprinkle body cavity with salt and pepper.

2. Wash parsley and shake well to dry; break into sprigs, discarding stems. Use to fill body cavity lightly. Secure neck skin to back of chicken with skewer; fold wings under, secure vent and truss legs in position.

3. In small mixing bowl, combine peach juice, lemon juice and soy sauce. Place chicken in roasting pan; pour peach juice mixture over chicken. Roast at 350° F for 1½ hours or until chicken is tender; baste frequently. Surround chicken with peaches; bake 10 minutes longer. Garnish with chicory if desired.

Serves 4. Shown on page 69.

⊗ *MoneySaving Tip:* Add eye and taste appeal to your budget entrees by arranging them in attractive serving dishes and dressing them up with garnishes. There's absolutely no need to buy special garnish ingredients—you probably have some in your refrigerator right now! Besides the traditional chicory and parsley sprigs, use the smaller leaves of salad greens, celery leaves, the tiniest leaves of young spinach, young beet leaves and bits of delicate carrot tops.

Barbecue-Baked Chicken

2½- to 3-pound broiler-fryer
  chicken, cut into serving pieces
½ cup butter or margarine
1 cup ketchup
½ cup water
½ cup chopped onion
¼ cup brown sugar
1 tablespoon vinegar
2 teaspoons Worcestershire
  sauce
¼ teaspoon garlic powder

1. Wash chicken pieces under cold running water; pat dry with paper towels. Melt butter or margarine in large skillet over medium heat; add chicken pieces and sauté for 10 minutes, turning to brown all sides. Place browned chicken in large casserole.

2. In small saucepan, combine ketchup, water, onion, brown sugar, vinegar, Worcestershire sauce and garlic powder; mix well. Simmer, uncovered, over low heat for 20 minutes, stirring occasionally.

3. Pour sauce over chicken pieces; turn chicken in sauce to coat well. Bake at 350° F for 45 minutes or until tender, turning twice.

Serves 4.

Deviled Chicken

2½- to 3-pound broiler-fryer
  chicken, cut into serving pieces
½ cup butter or margarine,
  melted
¼ cup ketchup
1 cup dry seasoned bread
  crumbs
1½ teaspoons dry mustard
½ teaspoon chili powder
½ teaspoon paprika
½ teaspoon salt

1. Wash chicken pieces under cold running water; pat dry with paper towels. Mix together melted butter or margarine and ketchup; brush over chicken pieces to coat.

2. In large, clean brown paper or plastic bag, combine bread crumbs, dry mustard, chili powder, paprika and salt. Place chicken pieces two at a time in bag; shake to coat well.

3. Arrange chicken in lightly greased baking dish. Bake at 350° F for 45 minutes to 1 hour, until tender.

Serves 4.

◎ *MoneySaving Tip:* Buy whole broiler-fryers, which are often on sale, and cut them into serving pieces yourself. Using a pair of poultry shears or a very sharp knife, cut down the center from the neck cavity to the vent (the larger opening) through the breast bone. Spread the chicken open and cut from the neck to the vent through the backbone; the chicken will now be halved. Cut each half into 4 pieces—breast, wing and back, thigh and body, and drumstick.

Chicken Juliet

2½- to 3-pound broiler-fryer chicken, cut into serving pieces

2 tablespoons vegetable oil

2 tablespoons butter or margarine

one 10¾-ounce can chicken broth

1 cup uncooked long-grain rice

1 cup sliced mushrooms

1 cup chopped onion

1 large orange, peeled, sectioned and chopped

½ cup coarsely chopped pecans or walnuts

1. Wash chicken under cold running water; pat dry with paper towels. Heat oil and butter or margarine in large skillet over medium heat; add chicken pieces and sauté for about 15 minutes, turning to brown all sides. Remove from skillet and set aside.

2. Add chicken broth to drippings in skillet, stirring to blend. Stir in rice, mushrooms, onion and orange. Cook for 5 minutes, stirring constantly. Stir in pecans or walnuts.

3. Spoon rice mixture into lightly greased 1½-quart casserole; place chicken pieces on top of rice. Cover casserole and bake at 350° F for 45 minutes or until chicken is tender.

Serves 4.

Luau Chicken

3-pound broiler-fryer chicken, cut into serving pieces

3 tablespoons vegetable oil

3 tablespoons butter or margarine

1½ cups chopped onions

one 20-ounce can pineapple chunks

¼ cup lemon juice

¼ cup ketchup

1 tablespoon brown sugar

1 tablespoon prepared spicy mustard

1 tablespoon soy sauce

1. Wash chicken pieces under cold running water; pat dry with paper towels. Heat oil and butter or margarine in large skillet over medium heat; add chicken pieces and sauté for about 15 minutes, turning to brown all sides. Remove from skillet and set aside.

2. Add onions to drippings in skillet; sauté until tender, about 4 minutes, stirring constantly. Stir in undrained pineapple, lemon juice, ketchup, brown sugar, mustard and soy sauce. Reduce heat to low and simmer for 5 minutes, stirring occasionally.

3. Place chicken in lightly greased 1½-quart casserole. Pour sauce over chicken; cover tightly. Bake at 350° F for 45 minutes or until chicken is tender.

Serves 4.

Skillet Chicken and Tarragon Rice

2½- to 3-pound broiler-fryer chicken, cut into serving pieces
½ cup flour
3 tablespoons vegetable oil
3 tablespoons butter or margarine
1 cup uncooked long-grain rice
1 cup sliced onion
1 cup dry white wine
1 cup chicken broth
1 teaspoon salt
1 teaspoon crumbled tarragon
½ teaspoon pepper

1. Wash chicken pieces under cold running water; pat dry with paper towels. Place flour in large, clean brown paper or plastic bag; add chicken pieces a few at a time and shake to coat well.

2. Heat oil and butter or margarine in large skillet over medium heat; add chicken pieces and sauté for about 15 minutes, turning to brown all sides. Remove from skillet and set aside.

3. Stir rice, onion, wine, chicken broth, salt, tarragon and pepper into drippings in skillet; blend well. Return chicken to skillet and reduce heat to low; cover and simmer for 40 minutes or until chicken and rice are tender.

Serves 4.

Simple Savory Chicken

2½- to 3-pound broiler fryer chicken, cut into serving pieces
¼ cup vegetable oil
½ cup chopped onion
½ cup chopped green pepper
½ cup sliced mushrooms
½ teaspoon salt
½ teaspoon oregano
1 cup dry white wine or chicken broth

1. Wash chicken pieces under cold running water; pat dry with paper towels. Heat oil in large skillet over medium heat; add chicken pieces and sauté for 10 minutes, turning to brown all sides. Remove from skillet and set aside.

2. Add onion, green pepper and mushrooms to drippings in skillet; sauté until onion is golden, about 5 minutes, stirring constantly.

3. Reduce heat to low; stir in salt, oregano and wine or chicken broth. Place chicken pieces on top of vegetables; simmer, covered, for 30 minutes.

4. Place chicken pieces on serving platter; keep warm. Simmer pan liquid, uncovered, until slightly thickened, stirring to puree vegetables in liquid. Pour over chicken.

Serves 4.

Chicken Spanish Style

2½- to 3-pound broiler-fryer chicken, cut into serving pieces

2 tablespoons vegetable oil

2 tablespoons butter or margarine

1 cup chopped onion

1 clove garlic, crushed

one 8-ounce can tomato sauce

½ cup sliced pitted black olives

1½ teaspoons grated lemon rind

½ teaspoon oregano

2 cups chicken broth

1. Wash chicken pieces under cold running water; pat dry with paper towels. Heat oil and butter or margarine in large skillet over medium heat; add chicken pieces and sauté for about 15 minutes, turning to brown all sides. Remove from skillet and set aside.

2. Add onion and garlic to drippings in skillet; sauté until onion is tender, about 4 minutes, stirring constantly. Stir in tomato sauce, olives, lemon rind and oregano; blend well.

3. Stir in chicken broth. Return chicken to skillet; reduce heat to low and simmer, covered, for 45 minutes or until chicken is tender.

Serves 4.

Chicken in White Wine

2½- to 3-pound broiler-fryer chicken, quartered

½ cup flour

½ teaspoon crumbled tarragon

½ cup butter or margarine

1 tablespoon olive or vegetable oil

8 cups thickly sliced mushrooms

2 shallots, finely chopped, or ¼ cup finely chopped onion

1 cup dry white wine

1. Wash chicken quarters under cold running water; pat dry with paper towels. In large, clean brown paper or plastic bag, combine flour and tarragon. Shake chicken pieces one at a time in bag to coat.

2. Heat butter or margarine and oil in large skillet over medium heat; add chicken pieces and sauté for about 10 minutes, turning to brown all sides. Remove chicken and set aside.

3. Add mushrooms and shallots or onion to drippings in skillet; toss well. Sauté, covered, until just tender, about 10 minutes, stirring occasionally to prevent sticking.

4. Reduce heat to low; add chicken and wine to skillet. Simmer, covered, for 45 minutes or until chicken is tender.

Serves 4.

Chicken Rolls Cordon Bleu

2 whole chicken breasts
4 slices precooked ham
4 slices Swiss cheese
½ cup butter or margarine
1 egg, beaten
1 cup dry unseasoned bread
  crumbs
¼ cup vegetable oil
one 7½-ounce can mushroom
  soup
½ cup sour cream
¼ cup dry white wine

1. Wash chicken breasts under cold running water; pat dry with paper towels. With small, sharp knife, remove bones from each breast. Cut breasts in half; place each half between two sheets of waxed paper and pound to ¼-inch thickness with wooden mallet or rolling pin. Remove and discard paper.

2. Place a ham slice, a cheese slice and 1 tablespoon of the butter or margarine on each chicken piece. Roll up jelly-roll fashion; secure both ends and seam with toothpicks.

3. Pour beaten egg onto one plate; place bread crumbs on second plate. Dip each roll in beaten egg to coat; drain slightly, then roll in bread crumbs to coat completely. Chill for 15 to 20 minutes to firm coating.

4. Heat remaining ¼ cup butter or margarine and the oil in medium skillet over medium heat; add chicken rolls and sauté, turning to brown all sides. Reduce heat to low and cook, covered, for 30 minutes, turning frequently. Place rolls on serving platter; keep warm.

5. Pour drippings from skillet. Add mushroom soup, sour cream and wine to skillet. Heat, stirring constantly, but do not boil. Serve over or alongside chicken rolls.

Serves 4.

◎ *MoneySaving Tip:* Boned chicken breasts, also sold as chicken cutlets, can be expensive; it's an easy matter to bone breasts yourself. Place the whole breast bone side down on a board or other flat surface; press down hard on the center of the breast with the palm of your hand to release the center bone from the flesh. Turn the breast bone side up and pull out the center bone. Using the tip of a small sharp knife, cut with short sharp strokes between the ribs and flesh to remove the rib bones. Cut out the neck bones at the top of the breast in the same way. Finally, cut the breast in half down the center to make 2 serving-size pieces. Don't throw away those bones—save them for soup!

Crisp Chicken Gratiné

4 chicken breast halves, skinned

½ cup butter or margarine

1 clove garlic, split

1 cup dry seasoned bread crumbs

½ cup grated sharp Cheddar cheese

¼ cup grated Parmesan cheese

1. Wash chicken under cold running water; pat dry with paper towels. Set chicken aside.

2. Melt butter or margarine in small saucepan over medium heat; add garlic and sauté for 1 minute. Remove and discard garlic.

3. In large bowl, combine bread crumbs with Cheddar and Parmesan cheese. Brush chicken breast halves with some melted butter or margarine; dip into bread crumb mixture to coat well.

4. Place chicken in large baking dish; drizzle with leftover butter or margarine. Bake at 350° F for 45 minutes or until chicken is tender, crisp and brown.

Serves 4.

Chicken in Mushroom-Shrimp Sauce

4 chicken breast halves, skinned, or 4 chicken legs and thighs, skinned

¼ cup vegetable oil

1 teaspoon crumbled tarragon

one 10¾-ounce can cream of shrimp soup

½ cup dry sherry or white wine

2 cups thinly sliced mushrooms

1. Wash chicken under cold running water; pat dry with paper towels. In large bowl, mix oil and tarragon; dip chicken in mixture to coat well.

2. Place chicken in large baking dish; bake at 350° F for 45 minutes to 1 hour or until crisp and golden, basting occasionally.

3. Meanwhile, combine soup, sherry or white wine and mushrooms in large bowl. Drain surplus fat from chicken; pour sauce over chicken. Return to oven and bake 15 minutes longer.

Serves 4.

MoneySaving Tip: Since chicken adapts readily to a wide range of seasonings, don't buy special herbs for a particular chicken dish—use what's on hand. Avoid only those seasonings with very heavy flavors that will mask the delicate chicken taste—a too-hearty sprinkling of oregano, for example, would overwhelm the chicken. If you're out of tarragon, the traditional seasoning for chicken, finely crumbled parsley flakes or basil will fill the seasoning bill.

Crisp Oven-Fried Chicken Breasts

6 chicken breast halves

1 egg

2 tablespoons water

1 clove garlic, crushed

1 cup dry unseasoned bread crumbs

1 tablespoon grated Parmesan cheese

1 teaspoon basil

1 teaspoon oregano

½ teaspoon garlic powder

⅓ cup butter or margarine, melted

1. Wash chicken under cold running water; pat dry with paper towels. Set aside.

2. In large bowl, beat together egg, water and garlic; set aside. In large, clean brown paper or plastic bag, combine bread crumbs, grated cheese, basil, oregano and garlic powder. Dip chicken breast halves in egg mixture, then shake, two at a time, in bread crumb mixture to coat.

3. Coat bottom of 13 x 9 x 2-inch baking dish with a little of the melted butter or margarine. Place chicken breasts bone side down in pan; drizzle with remaining butter or margarine. Bake at 350° F for 40 to 50 minutes or until crisp and golden, basting with pan juices. Do not baste during last 15 minutes of cooking time.

Serves 4 to 6.

Tangy Yogurt Chicken

4 chicken breast halves

4 chicken drumsticks

1 cup unflavored yogurt

1 cup packaged crushed herb stuffing mix

one 10¾-ounce can cream of chicken soup

½ cup milk

1. Wash chicken parts under cold running water; pat dry with paper towels. In large bowl, combine chicken parts and yogurt; toss to coat chicken well. Cover and refrigerate for at least 2 hours or overnight.

2. Remove chicken from yogurt; reserve yogurt. Roll chicken pieces in crushed stuffing mix; place in large baking dish. Bake at 350° F for 30 minutes; turn and bake 15 minutes longer, until crisp and tender.

3. In small saucepan, combine chicken soup, milk and reserved yogurt. Simmer over low heat for 5 minutes; do not boil. Serve sauce over chicken.

Serves 4.

Shanghai Drumsticks

8 chicken drumsticks
¼ cup honey
¼ cup soy sauce
¼ cup orange juice
¼ cup sherry
½ cup finely chopped onion
1 clove garlic, crushed

1. Wash chicken under cold running water; pat dry with paper towels. Prick chicken with fork.

2. In shallow baking dish, combine honey, soy sauce, orange juice, sherry, onion and garlic. Add chicken, turning to coat completely in mixture. Cover and refrigerate for at least 2 hours or overnight, turning occasionally.

3. Bake chicken in marinade, covered, at 350° F for 25 minutes; remove cover and bake 20 minutes longer.

Serves 4.

Almond Chicken and Rice

1 cup uncooked long-grain rice
2 chicken bouillon cubes
⅓ cup butter or margarine
⅓ cup slivered almonds
¼ cup thinly sliced green onion
2 cups cubed cooked chicken, or 1 pound precooked chicken roll, cubed
¼ cup chopped parsley

1. Cook rice according to label directions, adding chicken bouillon cubes to water.

2. Meanwhile, melt butter or margarine in large skillet over low heat. Add almonds and onions and sauté until golden, about 5 minutes. Stir in chicken; sauté 5 minutes longer, stirring constantly.

3. Add hot cooked rice to skillet; toss gently to mix with almond-chicken mixture. Stir in parsley.

Serves 4.

MoneySaving Tip: Even when purchased from a delicatessen, precooked chicken or turkey roll is a good buy. The boneless meat, which contains no fat, is pressed into a roll and steam-roasted. Look for frozen turkey or chicken rolls in the meat case, and prepare them as the label directs to have on hand for any dish that requires precooked chicken or turkey. Once you've prepared it, the meat roll will keep for up to 3 days in the refrigerator.

Oven-Baked Turkey Drumsticks

4 turkey drumsticks
½ cup flour
1 clove garlic, crushed
1 teaspoon seasoned salt
1 teaspoon crumbled tarragon
¼ cup vegetable oil
½ cup chicken broth

1. Wash turkey drumsticks under cold running water; pat dry with paper towels. In large, clean brown paper or plastic bag, combine flour, garlic, salt and tarragon. Add drumsticks two at a time; shake to coat well.

2. Heat oil in large skillet over medium heat; add drumsticks and sauté for about 5 to 7 minutes, turning to brown all sides.

3. Place turkey in 8 x 8 x 2-inch baking dish; add chicken broth. Cover dish tightly with foil. Bake at 350° F for 1½ hours or until drumsticks are tender.

Serves 4.

Turkey-Artichoke Casserole

6 slices bacon
1 cup chopped onion
1 clove garlic, crushed
3 cups diced cooked turkey, or 1½ pounds precooked turkey roll, diced
one 10-ounce package frozen artichoke hearts
one 10¼-ounce can beef gravy
¼ cup dry sherry

1. Fry bacon in large skillet over medium heat until crisp. Drain on paper towels; crumble and set aside.

2. Add onion and garlic to bacon fat in skillet; sauté until onion is tender, about 4 minutes, stirring constantly. Stir in turkey, artichoke hearts and beef gravy.

3. Simmer, covered, over low heat until artichoke hearts are tender, about 10 minutes; stir occasionally. Stir in sherry. Serve over crisp, hot toast points.

Serves 4.

Turkey Continental

1 cup uncooked long-grain rice

2 tablespoons butter or margarine

2 tablespoons vegetable oil

1 cup chopped onion

2 cups diced cooked turkey, or 1 pound precooked turkey roll, diced

1 cup peeled chopped tomatoes

one 8-ounce can string beans, drained

½ cup dry white wine

1. Cook rice according to label directions; keep warm.

2. Meanwhile, heat butter or margarine and oil in large skillet over medium heat. Add onion and sauté until tender, about 4 minutes, stirring constantly.

3. Add turkey, tomatoes, drained beans and wine. Reduce heat to low and simmer, covered, for 3 to 4 minutes or until turkey is heated through; serve over rice.

Serves 4.

Turkey Waldorf Salad

3 cups diced cooked turkey, or 1½ pounds precooked turkey roll, diced

1 cup diced apple

½ cup coarsely chopped walnuts

½ cup unflavored yogurt

1 to 2 teaspoons curry powder

1 small head Boston lettuce

2 large tomatoes

2 stalks celery

1. In medium bowl, combine turkey, apple, walnuts and yogurt; blend in curry to taste. Cover and chill for at least 1 hour.

2. Arrange lettuce leaves on each of 4 large salad platters. Cut each tomato into 8 wedges and celery into julienne strips.

3. Mound one-fourth of turkey mixture in center of each plate; surround with tomato wedges and celery strips.

Serves 4.

🛟 *MoneySaving Tip:* Fresh ground turkey can currently be found in the meat department in many parts of the country. A budget alternative to hamburger, it contains little or no fat, so is invariably a good buy. Use it as you would ground beef, but because it is so lean, sauté it in a generous amount of butter or margarine (¼ cup per pound of turkey) and dress it up with a savory gravy or piquant sauce. If you haven't served your family a roast turkey lately but would like to concoct Turkey-Artichoke Casserole, Turkey Continental or Turkey Waldorf Salad, try sautéing some ground turkey in butter and substituting it for the precooked turkey called for in those recipes.

Turkey Goodbye

one 10-ounce package frozen patty shells

1 cup leftover stuffing

one 10¼-ounce can beef gravy

⅓ cup dry sherry or red wine

1 teaspoon poultry seasoning

¼ teaspoon tarragon

2 cups diced cooked turkey

1 cup thinly sliced mushrooms

2 tablespoons grated Parmesan cheese

2 tablespoons chopped parsley

1. Bake frozen patty shells according to label directions; cool slightly on wire rack. Remove lid and cooked pastry from center. Fill each cooked shell with a little leftover stuffing. Place on baking sheet in 325° F oven to keep warm.

2. Meanwhile, combine beef gravy, sherry or red wine, poultry seasoning and tarragon in medium saucepan; stir to blend well. Add turkey and mushrooms. Simmer, covered, over low heat until turkey is piping hot and mushrooms are tender, about 10 minutes.

3. To serve, spoon turkey mixture into and over warm patty shells; sprinkle each with a little grated cheese and parsley.

Serves 4.

Hearty Homemade Turkey Soup

bones, meat, gravy and stuffing from leftover turkey

one 8-ounce can tomato sauce

1 cup chopped celery (with leaves)

1 cup chopped carrots

1 tablespoon salt

1 teaspoon poultry seasoning

1 teaspoon powdered thyme

1 large bay leaf

1 cup uncooked long-grain rice

¼ cup chopped parsley

1. Crush turkey bones into pieces; place in 8-quart saucepan along with any leftover turkey meat, gravy and stuffing. Add water to cover (approximately 8 cups).

2. Stir in tomato sauce; add celery, carrots, salt, poultry seasoning, thyme and bay leaf. Bring to boiling point over medium heat. Reduce heat to low and simmer, covered, for 2 hours.

3. Cool soup so bones and turkey meat may be handled with ease. Discard bones; dice meat and return to saucepan. Add rice; simmer, covered, over low heat for 20 to 30 minutes or until rice is tender. Stir in parsley.

Serves 4 to 6.

Broiled Crisp Flounder

½ cup butter or margarine, softened

1 clove garlic, crushed

2 tablespoons chopped parsley

1 teaspoon crumbled tarragon

1 teaspoon grated lemon rind

4 flounder fillets, fresh or frozen and thawed (about 1½ pounds)

½ cup flour

2 tablespoons olive oil

2 tablespoons butter or margarine

½ cup dry seasoned bread crumbs

1. Preheat broiler.

2. In small bowl, blend together softened butter or margarine, garlic, parsley, tarragon and lemon rind. Set aside.

3. Wipe fish with damp paper towels; sprinkle fish with flour to coat. Heat oil and butter or margarine in large skillet over medium heat; add fish fillets and sauté until golden brown, 3 minutes per side, turning carefully with broad spatula. Drain on paper towels.

4. Place fillets in 13 x 9 x 2-inch baking dish. Sprinkle with bread crumbs; dot with herb-butter mixture. Broil 6 inches from heat or until butter melts into crumbs and topping is deep brown.

Serves 4.

Flounder in Lemon Wine Sauce

4 flounder fillets, fresh or frozen and thawed (about 1½ pounds)

½ cup flour

¼ cup butter or margarine

2 tablespoons olive oil

2 tablespoons lemon juice

2 tablespoons dry white wine

2 tablespoons chopped parsley

1. Wipe fish with damp paper towels; sprinkle with flour to coat. Heat 2 tablespoons of the butter or margarine and the oil in large skillet over medium heat; add fish fillets and sauté until golden brown, 3 minutes per side, turning carefully with broad spatula. Drain on paper towels; place on hot serving platter and keep warm.

2. Add remaining butter or margarine to skillet; add lemon juice, wine and parsley. Bring quickly to boiling point; pour over fish fillets. Serve immediately.

Serves 4.

Ⓛ *MoneySaving Tip:* Flounder too expensive for your weekly food budget? Look for any white fish fillet as a substitute. Cod, haddock or whiting could be on sale this week and would make good stand-ins. Although they're seasonally economical, don't use mackerel, lake trout or bluefish in place of flounder—all are much more oily than the other white fish mentioned above.

Creamy Haddock in Celery Sauce

two 16-ounce packages frozen haddock fillets, partially thawed

2 tablespoons butter or margarine, melted

one 10¾-ounce can cream of celery soup

⅓ cup dry sherry

¼ teaspoon curry powder

¼ cup slivered almonds

1. Separate haddock fillets; wipe each with damp paper towels. Pour melted butter or margarine into large shallow baking pan. Add fish and turn to coat fillets evenly.

2. In small bowl, blend celery soup, sherry and curry; pour over fish. Sprinkle with slivered almonds. Bake at 350° F for 15 to 20 minutes or until fish flakes easily when tested with fork.

Serves 4 to 6.

Stuffed Cod Portugaise

1 small whole codfish or 1 center cut of cod (about 2 pounds)

STUFFING

1 cup dry seasoned bread crumbs

1 tablespoon grated Parmesan cheese

1 clove garlic, crushed

1 teaspoon basil

1 teaspoon oregano

2 tablespoons olive oil

1 egg, beaten

SAUCE

½ cup olive oil

2 cloves garlic, crushed

one 20-ounce can peeled tomatoes in puree

¼ cup red wine

½ teaspoon oregano

1. Wipe cod with damp paper towels; set cod aside.

2. To make stuffing, combine bread crumbs, grated cheese, 1 clove crushed garlic, the basil and 1 teaspoon oregano in medium bowl. Stir in 2 tablespoons oil and beaten egg with fork. Fill body cavity of fish with stuffing; place fish in greased 13 x 9 x 2-inch baking dish.

3. To make sauce, heat ½ cup oil in medium saucepan over low heat; add 2 cloves crushed garlic and sauté for 2 minutes. Stir in tomatoes, wine and ½ teaspoon oregano. Simmer, covered, for 10 minutes, stirring to break up tomatoes. Pour sauce over and around fish.

4. Tightly cover baking dish with foil. Bake at 350° F for 20 to 30 minutes or until fish flakes easily when tested with fork.

Serves 4.

Savory Baked Fillets

1½ pounds frozen fish fillets
   (flounder, perch or haddock),
   thawed
¼ cup butter or margarine
1 cup thinly sliced mushrooms
¾ cup chopped green pepper
½ cup chopped tomato
¼ cup dry white wine
½ teaspoon garlic salt
½ teaspoon basil

1. Wipe thawed fish with damp paper towels. Place fish in lightly greased 13 x 9 x 2-inch baking dish.

2. Melt butter or margarine in medium skillet over low heat; add mushrooms, green pepper and tomato and sauté until tender, about 5 minutes. Stir in wine, garlic salt and basil

3. Spoon vegetables over fish. Cover dish and bake at 350° F for 30 minutes, until fish flakes easily when tested with fork.

Serves 4.

Fish in Cream-Wine Sauce

one 16-ounce package frozen
   fillets (whiting, cod, haddock
   or sole), partially thawed
2 tablespoons butter or
   margarine
2 tablespoons chopped parsley
1 cup dry white wine
one 10¾-ounce can cream of
   chicken soup

1. Separate fish fillets; wipe each well with damp paper towels. Place fish in lightly greased 13 x 9 x 2-inch baking dish. Dot with butter or margarine; sprinkle with parsley. Pour wine over fish.

2. Bake at 375° F for 15 to 20 minutes or until fish flakes easily when tested with fork. Using slotted spatula, lift fish from cooking liquid to heated serving platter; keep warm.

3. In small saucepan, whisk together cooking liquid and chicken soup. Heat over medium heat until very hot; pour a little over fish and serve remaining sauce alongside.

Serves 4.

Fishburgers

one 16-ounce package frozen breaded fish fillets (4 fillets)

4 hamburger buns

2 tablespoons mayonnaise

2 tablespoons prepared mild mustard

4 thin slices onion

4 slices tomato

2 large slices Muenster cheese, halved

4 slices bacon, fried and crumbled

1. Cook fish fillets according to label directions. Preheat broiler.

2. Split hamburger buns and spread each cut side with mixture of mayonnaise and mustard. Place a cooked fillet on bottom half of each hamburger bun; top each with an onion and tomato slice and half a cheese slice.

3. Broil 6 inches from heat until cheese is melted, about 5 minutes. Sprinkle each burger with crumbled bacon and top with remaining hamburger bun half.

Serves 4.

⊗ *MoneySaving Tip:* To get the best possible flavor per dollar invested, thaw frozen fish only enough to separate the fillets. Cook the fish while it's still icy cold, before it's completely thawed. Don't thaw fish at room temperature; instead, thaw it in the package in the refrigerator for 4 to 6 hours. If you have a microwave oven, put the frozen fillets in it for 1 minute (many models have a "thaw" setting). Never thaw frozen fish under running water—this results in a good deal of flavor loss. Wipe all raw fish—whether it's fresh or has been frozen—with damp paper towels before you cook it, and cook it immediately after it's been thawed. Frozen breaded fish fillets, which are called for in the Fishburgers, above, don't require any thawing before they're cooked; in fact, they should go directly from your freezer to the cooking dish.

Sardine Supper

3 tablespoons olive oil
1½ cups chopped onions
1 cup chopped fresh tomatoes
1 clove garlic, crushed
one 8-ounce can tomato sauce
½ cup dry white wine
two 15-ounce cans sardines in
 tomato sauce
4 large slices whole wheat
 bread, toasted

1. Heat oil in medium saucepan over medium heat; add onions, tomatoes and garlic and sauté until tender, about 5 minutes, stirring constantly.

2. Stir in tomato sauce and wine. Reduce heat to low and simmer, covered, for 20 minutes, stirring occasionally.

3. Preheat broiler.

4. In small bowl, mash sardines until fine; spread over toasted bread. Broil 6 inches from heat for 3 to 5 minutes, until bubbling. Top each with a little sauce.

Serves 4.

Squid Salad Vinaigrette

3 pounds frozen squid, thawed
 and cleaned
2 tablespoons vinegar
6 parsley sprigs
½ cup olive oil
¼ cup lemon juice
¼ cup chopped parsley
2 cloves garlic, crushed

1. Cut squid tubes into ¼-inch rings; discard body of squid. Place rings in large saucepan; add vinegar, parsley sprigs and water to cover. Bring to boiling point over medium heat. Reduce heat to low and simmer, covered, for 45 minutes.

2. Remove squid from pan with slotted spoon and place in large serving bowl. Toss with oil, lemon juice, chopped parsley and garlic. Cover and chill overnight. If all dressing has been absorbed, add 3 tablespoons olive oil and 1 tablespoon lemon juice before serving.

Serves 4.

MoneySaving Tip: No squid in the market? The nearest budget substitute is un-fishy tripe, which can be cut into julienne strips, simmered in salted water until tender, and tossed with dressing. If tripe doesn't appeal to you, try cutting any fish into julienne strips and simmering the strips until tender (no more than 3 to 4 minutes) in water to cover that's been seasoned with a little vinegar; drain, then toss the fish with the vinaigrette dressing used in the above recipe.

Salmon Mousse Pie

one 9- to 11-ounce package
  piecrust mix
1 envelope unflavored gelatin
1¼ cups chicken broth or water
½ cup mayonnaise
one 7¾-ounce can salmon,
  drained and flaked
1 cup chopped, seeded, pared
  cucumber
¼ cup finely sliced green onion
2 tablespoons chopped parsley
1 teaspoon celery seed

1. Preheat oven to 400° F.

2. Prepare piecrust mix according to label directions. Divide in half; wrap and refrigerate one portion for another use. Roll out remaining half to line 9-inch pie plate. Trim and flute edge of pastry. Line shell with foil or waxed paper; fill with beans, rice or special aluminum pellets. Bake for 8 minutes; remove filling and foil and bake shell 3 minutes longer. Set on wire rack to cool.

3. Meanwhile, sprinkle gelatin over ¼ cup of the chicken broth or water in small saucepan; let stand for 5 minutes to soften. Place over low heat until gelatin is dissolved. Stir in remaining chicken broth or water. Whisk in mayonnaise, beating until smooth.

4. In medium bowl, combine salmon, cucumber, green onion, parsley and celery seed. Add gelatin mixture. Chill until mixture is semi-set, about 1 hour.

5. Spoon mixture into baked pie shell. Chill until filling is firm, at least 1 hour.

Serves 4 to 6.

Crispy Tuna Hot Pot

two 7-ounce cans tuna, flaked
1 cup packaged crushed herb
  stuffing mix
½ cup chopped onion
½ cup chopped pimiento
one 10¾-ounce can cream of
  chicken soup
two 1½-ounce cans potato sticks

1. In large bowl, combine undrained, flaked tuna, crushed stuffing mix, onion and pimiento. Stir in chicken soup; blend well.

2. Spoon mixture into lightly greased 1½-quart casserole. Place potato sticks over top; cover casserole lightly with foil. Bake at 350° F for 20 minutes; remove foil and bake 10 minutes longer.

Serves 4.

Deviled Tuna

two 7-ounce cans tuna, drained
and flaked

1 cup salted cracker crumbs

1 cup stuffed green olive slices

½ cup chopped celery

2 eggs

⅓ cup butter or margarine,
melted and cooled

2 tablespoons prepared spicy
mustard

4 to 6 drops hot pepper sauce

1. In medium bowl, combine tuna, cracker crumbs, olive slices and celery. In small bowl, beat together eggs, melted butter or margarine, mustard and hot pepper sauce.

2. Stir egg mixture into tuna mixture. Spoon mixture into lightly greased 1½-quart casserole. Bake at 350° F for 30 minutes or until hot and bubbling.

Serves 4.

Tuna-Green Bean Casserole

one 10-ounce package frozen
string beans

one 8-ounce package egg
noodles

one 11-ounce can Cheddar
cheese soup

one 7-ounce can tuna, drained
and flaked

½ cup chopped walnuts

½ cup chopped stuffed green
olives

1. Cook string beans according to label directions; drain and spread over bottom of lightly greased 2-quart casserole. Cook egg noodles according to label directions; drain and set aside.

2. Meanwhile, combine cheese soup, tuna, walnuts and olives in medium bowl. Stir in cooked noodles. Spoon mixture over green beans. Bake at 350° F for 20 to 30 minutes, until hot and bubbling.

Serves 4.

○ *MoneySaving Tip:* Even though tuna is not quite the bargain it used to be, a little tuna still goes a long way. Since it has no fat and no bone but a high level of protein, you truly get what you pay for. Keep a weather eye out for the best on-sale bargains. Tuna flakes are less expensive than the more common chunk-style or solid-pack tuna. White-meat canned tuna is the caviar of the tunafish world; water-packed tuna is less expensive (and contains fewer calories) than oil-packed tuna, which is more flavorful. Any can of tuna can be delectable when it's part of a salad, put into an antipasto or a casserole, or made into a savory sandwich filling.

Tuna Savoy

one and a half 16-ounce packages thin egg noodles

one 16-ounce container ricotta or small curd cottage cheese

3 eggs

¼ cup grated Parmesan cheese

1 teaspoon basil

two 7-ounce cans tuna, drained and flaked

1 cup thinly sliced mushrooms

1 cup sour cream

1. Cook egg noodles according to label directions; drain and measure 6 cups.

2. Using electric mixer at medium speed, beat ricotta or cottage cheese, two of the eggs, 2 tablespoons of the grated cheese and the basil in large bowl until smooth. Gently fold in cooked noodles, tuna and mushrooms.

3. Place mixture in lightly greased 2-quart casserole. Make topping by blending sour cream with remaining egg and grated cheese. Spoon over casserole. Bake at 350° F for 30 minutes.

Serves 4.

Tuna Tetrazzini

⅓ cup butter or margarine

½ cup finely chopped onion

⅓ cup flour

two 10¾-ounce cans chicken broth

1 cup half-and-half or light cream

¼ cup dry sherry

one 8-ounce package spaghettini

2 cups thinly sliced mushrooms

two 7-ounce cans tuna, drained and flaked

½ cup grated Parmesan cheese

1. Melt butter or margarine in large saucepan over medium heat; add onion and sauté until tender, about 5 minutes. Stir in flour and cook for 2 minutes, until bubbly.

2. Remove from heat; add chicken broth, half-and-half or cream and sherry, stirring to keep sauce smooth. Return sauce to heat; reduce heat to low and bring to boiling point, stirring until thickened.

3. Break spaghettini into 1-inch pieces; cook according to label directions until tender. Drain; stir into sauce along with mushrooms, tuna and grated cheese. Spoon into lightly greased 2-quart casserole; bake at 350° F for 30 minutes.

Serves 4.

Tuna and Biscuit Casserole

one 13-ounce can tuna, drained
and flaked

¼ cup chopped green onion

¼ cup mayonnaise

2 tablespoons pickle relish,
drained

2 cups prepared biscuit mix

one 11-ounce can Cheddar
cheese soup

⅓ cup milk

1. Preheat oven to 450° F.

2. Combine tuna, green onion, mayonnaise and drained pickle relish. Spread over bottom of lightly greased 8 x 8 x 2-inch baking dish.

3. Prepare biscuit mix according to label directions; spoon evenly over tuna mixture. Bake for 15 minutes.

4. Meanwhile, heat cheese soup and milk in small saucepan. Serve as sauce with casserole.

Serves 4.

Tuna-Cheese Quiche

one 9- to 11-ounce package
piecrust mix

2 tablespoons butter or
margarine

½ cup thinly sliced green
onions

2 tablespoons finely chopped
green pepper

one 7-ounce can oil-packed
tuna, drained and flaked

3 eggs

1 cup heavy cream

1 cup milk

2 tablespoons sherry

1 cup grated Swiss cheese

1. Preheat oven to 400° F.

2. Prepare piecrust mix according to label directions. Divide in half; wrap and refrigerate one portion for another use. Roll out remaining half to line 9-inch pie plate. Trim and flute edge of pastry. Line shell with foil or waxed paper; fill with beans, rice or special aluminum pellets. Bake for 8 minutes; remove filling and foil and bake shell 3 minutes longer. Set on wire rack to cool while making filling.

3. Melt butter or margarine in medium skillet over medium heat; add green onions and green pepper and sauté until tender, about 5 minutes. Remove from heat; gently stir in tuna. Spread mixture over bottom of baked pie shell.

4. In medium bowl, beat together eggs, cream, milk and sherry. Stir in grated cheese; pour mixture over tuna in pie shell.

5. Reduce oven heat to 375° F. Bake quiche for 30 to 35 minutes or until knife inserted in center comes out clean. Let stand on wire rack for 10 minutes before cutting.

Serves 4 to 6.

Tuna-Stuffed Tomatoes

4 large or 6 medium tomatoes

two 7-ounce cans tuna, drained
  and flaked

1 cup diced pared cucumber

¾ cup mayonnaise

⅓ cup chopped parsley

2 tablespoons lemon juice

1 teaspoon celery seed

½ teaspoon salt

1. Wash and dry tomatoes. Cut ½-inch slice off top of each to form a lid. Using a teaspoon, scoop out seeds and pulp, leaving a shell ¼ inch thick.

2. Chop tomato pulp; place in medium bowl. Stir in tuna, cucumber, mayonnaise, parsley, lemon juice, celery seed and salt; mix well.

3. Fill tomato shells with tuna mixture. Serve on bed of lettuce, with potato salad as accompaniment if desired.

Serves 4.

Iced Marinated Mussels

5 to 6 pounds fresh mussels

1½ cups dry white wine

½ cup water

1 cup olive or vegetable oil

¼ cup red wine vinegar

2 cloves garlic, crushed

1 tablespoon prepared Dijon-
  style or mild mustard

1 teaspoon sugar

1 teaspoon oregano

1 teaspoon tarragon

1. Scrub mussels thoroughly under cold running water with clean vegetable brush to remove beard. Discard any with open shells.

2. Place mussels in large heavy saucepan; add 1 cup of the wine and the water. Simmer, covered, over low heat until shells open wide, about 10 minutes. Uncover and let cool. Discard any with closed shells.

3. In large liquid measure, combine remaining ½ cup wine, the oil, vinegar, garlic, mustard, sugar, oregano and tarragon. Beat with fork or small whisk to blend well.

4. Remove top shells from mussels. Place mussels in large bowl and pour dressing over them; toss well and chill for at least 2 hours. Stir frequently. Serve in large bowls accompanied by hot crusty French bread.

Serves 4. Shown on page 70.

Note: Cherrystone clams may be used instead of mussels.

Clams Ramon

one 10-ounce package frozen
  patty shells
1 pint clams, shucked
dry white wine
¼ cup butter or margarine
¼ cup flour
1 cup thinly sliced mushrooms
½ cup grated Swiss cheese
½ teaspoon Worcestershire
  sauce

1. Bake patty shells according to label directions; set on wire rack to cool.

2. Cook clams in their liquid in medium saucepan over low heat until their edges begin to curl, about 5 minutes. Drain clam liquid into glass measure, adding enough wine to measure 2 cups. Remove cooked clams from pan and set aside.

3. Melt butter or margarine in same saucepan over medium heat. Stir in flour and cook for 2 minutes, until mixture bubbles, stirring constantly.

4. Remove pan from heat; slowly blend in clam liquid-wine mixture, stirring to keep smooth. Place over low heat; bring to boiling point, stirring constantly until mixture thickens. Stir in mushrooms; cook 3 minutes longer.

5. Stir in grated cheese, Worcestershire sauce and reserved clams. Spoon into patty shells.

Serves 4.

Note: Any shellfish may be used instead of clams.

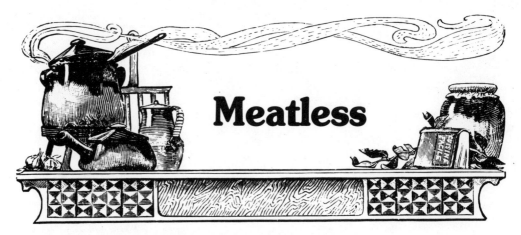

Meatless

BEANS, PASTA, RICE, EGGS AND CHEESE

This chapter is full of real dollar stretchers. Though calorie-conscious eaters tend to worry that starchy foods like beans, pasta and rice are "fattening," these economical, protein-packed carbohydrates actually contain half as many calories as pure fat and no more than pure protein. Furthermore, beans and enriched pasta and rice are chock-full of vitamins and minerals. For a full protein complement, combine them with meat, fish, eggs or cheese.

Discover the elegance of Black Bean Soup laced with sherry, the hearty goodness of Baked Lentils and Sausage. Or try some of the original or traditional pasta recipes included here—picky eaters will become your best customers when you serve dishes like Three-Cheese Spinach Noodles and Angry Macaroni for supper.

Eggs and cheese are excellent alternatives to meat. In fact, ounce for ounce, cheese has more protein than most steaks. And eggs lend themselves to an astounding variety of flavors and textures. For a change, you might like Double Creamy Eggs, rich with cheese and served over ham and toasted English muffins, or Ratatouille Omelet, stuffed with vegetables and spiced with the flavors of the Mediterranean.

For eating, buy the larger size eggs. For cooking, medium-size are perfectly adequate and much cheaper. Eggs should be kept refrigerated, and stored blunt end up.

You'll find cheese changes character according to the company it keeps. Tuck it in a crêpe and it's dressed for company. Bake it with corned beef hash and mashed potatoes and it's down-home family fare. Just be sure to follow the directions given for these dishes, because overcooked cheese tends to become tough and stringy.

So, for delicious, family-pleasing dinners, take your pick of these money-saving recipes.

Brazilian Black Beans

one 16-ounce bag black beans
¼ pound sliced bacon, cut into 1-inch pieces
2 cups chopped onions
2 cloves garlic, crushed
2 teaspoons salt
½ cup dry sherry
½ cup chopped parsley

1. Soak beans overnight in water to cover; drain. Place in large saucepan with water to cover; simmer, covered, over low heat for 2 hours or until just tender. Drain well.

2. Fry bacon in large skillet over medium heat until pieces curl slightly. Add onions, garlic and salt. Cook until onions are tender, about 6 to 8 minutes, stirring constantly. Stir in beans and sherry.

3. Reduce heat to low; cook until beans are heated through, about 5 minutes, stirring constantly. Place in serving dish and sprinkle with chopped parsley.

Serves 4 to 6.

Black Bean Soup

one 16-ounce bag black beans
8 cups water
1 ham bone
1 cup chopped onion
1 teaspoon salt
¼ cup sherry
2 hard-cooked eggs
lemon wedges

1. Wash beans well under cold running water; place in large saucepan with 8 cups water, the ham bone, onion and salt. Bring to boiling point over medium heat; skim any foam from surface. Reduce heat to low and simmer, covered, for 1½ to 2 hours or until beans are tender.

2. Remove ham bone from soup; cut off any lean meat and dice finely. Puree soup, 2 cups at a time, in blender; return to pan. Add diced ham; stir in sherry and heat 5 minutes over low heat.

3. Sieve hard-cooked egg yolks; chop whites finely. Sprinkle over soup as garnish. Serve lemon wedges for seasoning soup if desired.

Serves 4.

MoneySaving Tip: Black beans are a budget staple from the Caribbean, Latin America and Africa. Staunch, hearty and nutritious —especially when served with a little meat, eggs or fish—they have a warm rich flavor similar to that of red kidney beans.

Hearty Lima-Tomato Soup

one 16-ounce bag dried lima
  beans
one 32-ounce can Italian-style
  tomatoes, crushed
2 tablespoons olive oil
1 clove garlic, crushed
1 teaspoon salt
1 teaspoon basil
¼ teaspoon pepper
½ cup chopped parsley
½ cup grated Parmesan cheese

1. Soak lima beans overnight in water to cover; drain. Place in large saucepan with water to cover; simmer, covered, over low heat for 2 hours or until just tender. Drain well.

2. In large saucepan, combine cooked limas, tomatoes, oil, garlic, salt, basil and pepper. Simmer, covered, over low heat for 15 minutes.

3. Serve soup in large individual bowls; sprinkle with parsley and grated cheese.

Serves 4 to 6.

Traditional Three-Bean Salad

one 17-ounce can garbanzo
  beans (chick peas), drained
one 15½-ounce can red kidney
  beans, drained
one 15½-ounce can wax beans,
  drained
½ cup chopped parsley
½ cup vegetable oil
¼ cup red wine vinegar
1 clove garlic, crushed
1 teaspoon celery seed
1 teaspoon salt
¼ teaspoon pepper
1 head Boston lettuce

1. In large bowl, combine drained garbanzo, red kidney and wax beans. Toss with parsley.

2. In small bowl, beat together oil, vinegar, garlic, celery seed, salt and pepper. Pour over beans; toss well. Chill for at least 1 hour.

3. To serve, line salad bowl with washed and dried lettuce leaves. Toss beans once more and spoon into lettuce-lined bowl.

Serves 4.

⊕ *MoneySaving Tip:* Vary your diet by experimenting with all kinds of low-cost dried beans, peas and lentils. Follow package directions for rinsing and presoaking. Since these legumes are cooked for a long time over low heat, it's a good idea to check them every now and then to see if they need more liquid to prevent scorching. Any bean dish will be more flavorful if it's made ahead, chilled in the refrigerator and then reheated.

Baked Lentils and Sausage

one 16-ounce bag lentils
¾ pound sweet Italian-style sausages
¾ pound hot Italian-style sausages
1 cup chopped onion
2 cloves garlic, crushed
2 tablespoons prepared spicy mustard
½ cup chopped parsley

1. Place lentils in large saucepan with water to cover; simmer, covered, over low heat for 2 hours or until just tender. Drain well.

2. Prick sausages well with fork. Sauté sausages in large skillet over low heat until thoroughly cooked, about 15 to 20 minutes, turning to brown all sides. Remove from skillet and set aside.

3. Add onion and garlic to drippings in skillet; sauté until onion is tender, about 4 minutes, stirring constantly.

4. Stir in mustard and cooked lentils. Add sausages; heat, stirring occasionally, for about 5 minutes. Place in serving dish. Sprinkle with chopped parsley.

Serves 4 to 6.

Lentil Soup

2 cups lentils
10 cups water
1 ham bone
2 cups chopped onions
2 cloves garlic
2 bay leaves
2 to 3 tablespoons tomato paste
1 to 2 tablespoons red wine vinegar

1. Place lentils in large saucepan with 10 cups water and the ham bone. Bring to boiling point over medium heat; skim any foam from surface. Reduce heat to low and simmer, covered, for 1 hour.

2. Add onions, garlic and bay leaves. Cook 1 hour longer. Remove ham bone from soup; cut off any lean meat and dice finely. Remove and discard garlic and bay leaves.

3. Puree soup, 2 cups at a time, in blender; return to pan; add diced ham, tomato paste and vinegar. Heat for 5 minutes over low heat.

Serves 4.

Linguine in Garlic-Clam Sauce

¾ cup olive oil

one 12-ounce can minced clams, drained

½ cup chopped parsley

3 cloves garlic, crushed

one 16-ounce package linguine

freshly ground black pepper

1. In small saucepan, combine oil, drained clams, parsley and garlic. Heat over very low heat; do not fry.

2. Cook linguine according to label directions; drain. Place in hot serving bowl; toss with hot garlic-clam sauce. Grind black pepper over each serving and serve immediately.

Serves 4.

Angry Macaroni

½ cup olive oil

2 cloves garlic, finely chopped

one 6-ounce can tomato paste

one 32-ounce can Italian-style tomatoes

½ cup chopped pitted black olives

2 teaspoons red pepper flakes

1 teaspoon salt

1 teaspoon sugar

1 teaspoon basil

1 teaspoon oregano

one 16-ounce package macaroni

½ cup grated Parmesan cheese

1. Heat oil in medium saucepan over low heat; add garlic and sauté just until golden. Stir in tomato paste; cook for 5 minutes, stirring constantly.

2. Add undrained tomatoes, olives, red pepper flakes, salt, sugar, basil and oregano. Stir to mix well, breaking tomatoes into small pieces. Simmer over very low heat for 4 to 5 minutes, stirring occasionally to avoid scorching.

3. Meanwhile, cook macaroni according to label directions; drain. Place in large warm serving bowl; toss with grated cheese and top with sauce.

Serves 4.

◯ *MoneySaving Tip:* When a recipe calls for macaroni, don't feel bound to use everyday elbow macaroni—make a foray into the field of low-cost elbow alternatives. You'll find a wide assortment of shapes and sizes—and even a different color or two—on the shelves of your supermarket. Instead of the elbow type in dishes like Angry Macaroni and Macaroni Bake, choose ziti, mostaccioli or rigatoni, which are all tubular macaroni. Experiment with different shapes like bow ties, shells and corkscrews. Hearty whole wheat elbow macaroni, which used to be confined to health food stores, is now widely marketed. In other pasta departments, there are spinach noodles and spaghetti made from Jerusalem artichokes to add nutrition and flavor to your budget-wise menus.

Macaroni Bake

4 slices bacon

1½ cups uncooked elbow macaroni

1 egg

1½ cups milk

2 cups diced leftover meat (turkey, chicken, pork or ham)

1 cup grated Monterey Jack cheese

2 tablespoons grated onion

1 teaspoon salt

½ cup seasoned bread crumbs

2 tablespoons butter or margarine

1. Fry bacon in small skillet over medium heat until crisp. Drain on paper towels; crumble and set aside.

2. Cook macaroni according to label directions; drain. Meanwhile, beat together egg and milk in large bowl. Stir in cooked macaroni, meat, grated cheese, onion and salt.

3. Spoon mixture into lightly greased 2-quart casserole. Sprinkle top with bread crumbs and crumbled bacon; dot with butter or margarine. Bake at 350° F for 30 minutes.

Serves 4.

Note: This is an ideal dish for using leftover meat.

Macaroni Pie

one 8-ounce package macaroni

one 16-ounce container ricotta or small curd cottage cheese

3 eggs

½ cup grated Parmesan cheese

1 teaspoon garlic salt

1 teaspoon basil

½ teaspoon pepper

1. Cook macaroni according to label directions. Drain well.

2. Using electric mixer at medium speed, beat ricotta or cottage cheese, eggs, Parmesan cheese, garlic salt, basil and pepper in large bowl. Stir in macaroni.

3. Spoon mixture into a lightly greased 1-quart casserole. Bake at 350° F for 45 minutes.

Serves 4.

Alsatian Noodle Skillet Dinner

one 16-ounce package brown-and-serve herb-seasoned sausages

one 16-ounce can sauerkraut, drained

2 cups sliced unpeeled apples

½ cup dry white wine

1 tablespoon caraway seeds

one 16-ounce package egg noodles

1. Fry sausages in large skillet over low heat until thoroughly cooked, about 10 to 15 minutes, turning to brown all sides. Remove from skillet; set aside and keep warm.

2. Add drained sauerkraut, apple slices, wine and caraway seeds to drippings in skillet; toss to blend well. Cook, covered, for 10 minutes or until apples are just tender.

3. Meanwhile, cook noodles according to label directions just until tender; drain. Add to skillet along with sausages. Toss gently to blend; heat for 2 to 3 minutes.

Serves 4.

Noodle-Bacon Bake

one and a half 16-ounce packages thin egg noodles

6 slices bacon

1 cup chopped onion

2 cups thinly sliced mushrooms

1 cup grated sharp Cheddar cheese

one 10¾-ounce can cream of chicken soup

1. Cook noodles according to label directions; drain and measure 6 cups. Meanwhile, fry bacon in large skillet over medium heat until crisp. Drain on paper towels; crumble and set aside.

2. Add onions to bacon fat in skillet; sauté until tender, about 5 minutes. Add mushrooms to skillet and cook 3 minutes longer, stirring constantly.

3. Toss noodles with vegetables and grated cheese. Gently stir in chicken soup. Spoon mixture into lightly greased 2-quart casserole. Bake at 350° F for 20 to 30 minutes, until very hot and bubbly.

Serves 4.

Noodles with Herb Cream Cheese

8 slices bacon

one 16-ounce package egg
  noodles

2 eggs, beaten

two 4-ounce packages herb-
  flavored double cream cheese

1. Fry bacon in small skillet over medium heat until crisp. Drain on paper towels; crumble and set aside.

2. Cook noodles according to label directions; drain. Place in large bowl; toss with beaten eggs, cream cheese and bacon.

3. Spoon into lightly greased 1½-quart casserole. Bake at 350° F for 20 minutes.

Serves 4.

Three-Cheese Spinach Noodles

one 16-ounce package spinach
  noodles

2 eggs, beaten

2 tablespoons butter or
  margarine

1 cup grated Swiss cheese

1 cup grated provolone cheese

½ cup grated Romano or
  Parmesan cheese

freshly ground black pepper

1. Cook spinach noodles according to label directions; drain. Place in large heated serving bowl; immediately pour in beaten eggs and toss to coat noodles well.

2. Add butter or margarine; toss to mix well. Add grated Swiss, provolone and Romano or Parmesan cheese. Toss to mix well. Divide among 4 individual serving plates. Sprinkle with freshly ground black pepper.

Serves 4. Shown on page 71.

◎ *MoneySaving Tip:* Grating cheese yourself is far more economical than buying packages of pre-grated cheese, and carries a fringe benefit—more freshness for greater flavor! Cheese that has dried out slightly and so is less appealing for snacking and desserts is ideal for use in cooked dishes. Slightly dry cheese also grates more easily and to a finer consistency. Grate cheese right before using it in sauces or to top casseroles or pasta dishes. It's best to grate just enough for the dish you're preparing. However, if you miscalculate and have a surplus, wrap it in an airtight plastic bag to prevent further drying, and store it in the refrigerator.

Pasta with Beans

one 16-ounce can whole peeled
  tomatoes
2 cups water or chicken broth
½ cup olive oil
2 cloves garlic, crushed
one 20-ounce can white kidney
  beans
one 16-ounce package fine
  noodles, angel-hair style
½ cup chopped parsley
½ cup grated Parmesan cheese

1. In large saucepan, combine undrained tomatoes, water or chicken broth, oil and garlic. Using slotted spoon, crush tomatoes into small pieces against sides of pan.

2. Bring mixture to simmering point over low heat; cook, covered, for 45 minutes, stirring occasionally. Add undrained beans; cook 5 minutes longer.

3. Meanwhile, cook noodles according to label directions; drain and place in large warm bowl. Pour tomato sauce over noodles and toss to mix well. Serve in large soup bowls; sprinkle each serving with parsley and grated cheese.

Serves 4.

Rigatoni Castagna Style

one 16-ounce package rigatoni
¼ cup butter or margarine
2 tablespoons vegetable oil
3 cups sliced mushrooms
1 cup chopped Genoa salami
1 cup grated Romano or
  Parmesan cheese
½ cup heavy cream

1. Cook rigatoni according to label directions. Meanwhile, heat 2 tablespoons of the butter or margarine and the oil in a medium skillet over medium heat. Add mushrooms and salami and sauté until mushrooms are tender, about 8 to 10 minutes.

2. Drain rigatoni and place in heated serving bowl; toss with remaining 2 tablespoons butter or margarine. Add grated cheese and cream; toss to blend well.

3. Add cooked mushrooms and salami. Toss again to blend.

Serves 4.

   Ⓧ *MoneySaving Tip:* You'll get the most flavor and nutritive value for your money if you cook all spaghetti only until it is *al dente.* Test for this by pressing the pasta between your finger and thumb. If it gives a slight, "toothsome" resistance, it's al dente and ready to serve. It's always better to slightly undercook pasta than to overcook it, especially if it's going to be cooked further in a casserole.

Cheese and Spinach Stuffed Shells

one 16-ounce package large
pasta shells

one 10-ounce package frozen
chopped spinach

two 16-ounce containers ricotta
or small curd cottage cheese

1 cup grated mozzarella cheese

1 clove garlic, crushed

1 teaspoon basil

one 32-ounce jar spaghetti
sauce

1. Cook pasta shells according to label directions until just tender, about 10 minutes. Drain, and let cool enough to handle.

2. Meanwhile, cook spinach according to label directions. Drain in fine sieve, pressing out all water; cool.

3. In medium bowl, combine cooked spinach, ricotta or cottage cheese, mozzarella cheese, garlic and basil. Stuff cooked pasta shells with mixture.

4. Pour 3 cups of the spaghetti sauce into shallow 1½-quart baking dish. Set pasta shells filling side up in sauce; spoon remaining sauce over shells. Bake at 350° F for 30 minutes.

Serves 4 to 6.

Spaghetti Carbonara

1 pound sliced bacon

one 16-ounce package spaghetti

3 eggs, beaten

½ cup heavy cream

½ cup grated Parmesan cheese

freshly ground black pepper

1. Fry bacon in large skillet over medium heat until crisp. Drain on paper towels; crumble and set aside.

2. Cook spaghetti according to label directions; drain and place immediately in large heated serving bowl.

3. Pour in beaten eggs; toss for eggs to coat spaghetti and cook slightly. Add cream and grated cheese and toss quickly.

4. Toss in crumbled bacon. Grind black pepper over each serving and serve immediately.

Serves 4.

Note: This dish is best made with thin spaghetti or spaghettini.

Rice and Beans Jamaican Style

1 cup dried red kidney beans

1 cup uncooked long-grain rice

¼ cup vegetable oil

2 tablespoons finely chopped fresh ginger root, or
   2 teaspoons powdered ginger

1 teaspoon salt

3 to 4 drops hot pepper sauce

1. Soak kidney beans overnight in water to cover; drain. Place in large saucepan with water to cover; simmer, covered, over low heat for 2 hours or until just tender. Drain well.

2. Meanwhile, cook rice according to label directions. Toss together hot beans and hot rice in heated serving bowl.

3. Immediately toss with oil, ginger, salt and hot pepper sauce. Serve at once.

Serves 4.

Rice Genoese

1½ cups uncooked long-grain rice

4 slices bacon, cut into 1-inch pieces

1½ cups finely diced carrots

1½ cups finely chopped onions

¼ cup dry white wine

¼ cup olive oil

½ teaspoon pepper

1. Cook rice according to label directions. Meanwhile, fry bacon in large skillet over medium heat until pieces curl slightly. Add carrots and onions.

2. Reduce heat to low; cook vegetables until tender, about 8 to 10 minutes, stirring constantly. Add wine; cook, covered, 2 minutes longer.

3. Stir in rice, oil and pepper. Cook for 2 minutes or until mixture is very hot, stirring constantly.

Serves 4.

Rice Italian Style

¼ cup butter or margarine
1 cup chopped onion
2 cups uncooked long-grain rice
giblets from 2 chickens
4 cups water
4 cups chicken broth
1 cup chopped mushrooms
1 cup grated Parmesan cheese

1. Melt butter or margarine in large saucepan over medium heat; add onion and sauté until brown and tender, about 5 to 8 minutes. Add rice and sauté until golden brown, stirring constantly.

2. Wash giblets under cold running water; trim off and discard any fat. Add giblets to saucepan along with 4 cups water and the broth.

3. Bring to boiling point; reduce heat and simmer, covered, for 15 minutes, stirring frequently. Add mushrooms and ½ cup of the grated cheese; cook 5 minutes longer, stirring constantly. Rice should be creamy.

4. Carefully remove giblets from hot rice; dice meat finely and return to saucepan; mix well. Serve in individual bowls; sprinkle with remaining ½ cup grated cheese.

Serves 4.

🛟 *MoneySaving Tip:* Rice is an excellent buy both in terms of economics and nutrition. It comes in many varieties:

Long-grain rice is usually converted, which means it has been pre-processed to remove surplus surface starch; this speeds cooking and prevents stickiness. The nutrients lost in the processing are then replaced before the rice is sold.

Short-grain rice is commonly found in supermarkets that feature Latin American foods. Short-grain is not converted and the grains can stick together after cooking. It is slightly less expensive than long-grain.

Polished rice is milled until it is as white as possible, and processed to give the grains a high gloss.

Quick-cooking white rice has been completely (or almost completely) precooked, then dried. It can be reconstituted with boiling water, and requires very little preparation time.

Brown rice has been milled to remove only the outer hull; thus it retains its natural color and is the most nutritious of the rice grains.

Wild rice is not really a rice at all, but grass seeds that resemble rice grains. It is grown only in certain areas of the country. Wild rice is very expensive; except for occasional splurges, substitute brown and long-grain rice mixes for this luxury.

Rice-Stuffed Tomatoes

4 large or 6 medium tomatoes
1 cup uncooked long-grain rice
1 cup dry seasoned bread
  crumbs
½ cup chopped parsley
⅓ cup olive oil
1 clove garlic, crushed
½ teaspoon powdered thyme

1. Wash and dry tomatoes. Cut ½-inch slice off top of each to form a lid. Using a teaspoon, scoop out seeds and pulp, leaving a shell ¼ inch thick. Chop tomato pulp; set aside pulp and shells.

2. Cook rice according to label directions. Place in medium bowl. Combine with chopped tomato pulp, bread crumbs, parsley, oil, garlic and thyme; mix to blend well. Fill tomato shells with mixture.

3. Place stuffed tomatoes in lightly greased 8 x 8 x 2-inch baking dish. Bake at 350° F for 30 minutes. Serve hot as a vegetable, or chill and serve as a salad.

Serves 4.

Rice Salad Provençal

1½ cups uncooked long-grain
  rice
½ cup olive oil
¼ cup red wine vinegar
¼ cup chopped parsley
1 clove garlic, crushed
1 teaspoon salt
¼ teaspoon pepper
1 cup thinly sliced celery
1 cup thinly sliced cucumber
1 cup thin tomato wedges

1. Cook rice according to label directions; while hot, toss with oil, vinegar, parsley, garlic, salt and pepper. Chill for at least 2½ hours.

2. Just before serving, toss rice with celery, cucumber and tomato. If salad is not moist, toss in an additional 2 tablespoons olive oil and 1 tablespoon vinegar.

Serves 4.

MoneySaving Tip: Hard-cooked eggs can be a budgetary mainstay in your kitchen for use in salads and entrées. Hard-cook them the right way, though, or they may be watery and difficult to shell. Pierce the blunt end of the egg with a needle and place the egg in salted water to cover. Simmer, covered, for 15 minutes, then plunge it into cold water just until it's cool enough to handle. Crack the shell and peel it off. Return the egg to cold water to cool completely. If you want to store the eggs, cool them in cold water in the shell, refrigerate, and shell them under cold running water when ready to use.

Double Creamy Eggs

2 cups light cream or half-and-half

one 8-ounce package cream cheese, cut into pieces

1 cup grated American cheese

6 hard-cooked eggs, sliced

1 clove garlic, crushed

6 English muffins

6 slices precooked ham

1. Bring cream or half-and-half just to boiling point in top of double boiler over medium heat. Add cream cheese; stir to melt. Add grated American cheese; stir to melt. Gently stir in eggs; place over simmering water and keep warm.

2. Split and toast English muffins; place 2 halves side by side on individual platters. Top with ham slice. Spoon cheese-egg mixture over ham.

Serves 6.

Eggs Chantilly

6 slices bacon

1 cup chopped onion

1 cup thinly sliced mushrooms

8 hard-cooked eggs, cut lengthwise in half

2 cups grated sharp Cheddar cheese

one 10¾-ounce can cream of celery soup

½ cup milk

¼ cup sherry

one 8-ounce package refrigerator biscuits

1. Preheat oven to 375° F.

2. Fry bacon in medium skillet over medium heat until crisp. Drain on paper towels; crumble and set aside.

3. Add onion to bacon fat in skillet; sauté until tender, about 5 minutes. Add mushrooms and sauté 3 to 4 minutes longer.

4. Spread vegetables over bottom of lightly greased 13 x 9 x 2-inch baking dish; arrange egg halves cut side up over vegetables. Sprinkle with grated cheese.

5. In small bowl, combine celery soup, milk and sherry. Pour over eggs. Arrange refrigerator biscuits on top of sauce. Bake for 20 minutes, until biscuits are golden brown.

Serves 4.

Sausage and Egg Frittata

2 tablespoons butter or
margarine
2 tablespoons vegetable oil
1½ cups diced peeled potatoes
1 cup chopped onion
1 clove garlic, crushed
1 pound sweet Italian-style
sausages
8 eggs
1 teaspoon red pepper flakes

1. Heat butter or margarine and oil in large skillet over medium heat; add potatoes, onion and garlic and sauté until golden, about 5 minutes, stirring constantly.

2. Remove meat from sausage casings and crumble meat into skillet with vegetables. Cook until sausage is browned and well done, about 15 minutes, stirring occasionally.

3. In small bowl, beat together eggs and red pepper flakes. Pour into skillet; reduce heat to low. Cook, stirring constantly, until eggs are slightly thickened.

4. Continue to cook without stirring until underside is golden and top surface is shiny and moist. Cut into wedges to serve.

Serves 4.

Ratatouille Omelet

¼ cup vegetable oil
1 cup chopped onion
2 cups chopped unpeeled
eggplant
1 cup chopped zucchini
1 cup chopped tomatoes
2 teaspoons basil
½ teaspoon oregano
6 eggs
2 tablespoons water
2 tablespoons grated Parmesan
cheese
2 tablespoons butter or
margarine

1. Heat oil in large skillet over medium heat; add onion and sauté until transparent, about 3 minutes. Add eggplant, zucchini and tomatoes; cook until eggplant is golden and tender, about 8 minutes, stirring constantly. Add basil and oregano; mix well. Set aside and keep warm.

2. Beat together eggs, water and grated cheese. Melt butter or margarine in another large skillet over medium heat. Add egg mixture; stir vigorously until eggs just begin to thicken; reduce heat to low. Stir eggs once more, then continue cooking until eggs are set but moist on top.

3. Place vegetables on one side of omelet; using large spatula, fold over omelet to cover filling. Slide onto serving platter.

Serves 4. Shown on page 72.

Luncheon Omelet Versailles

8 **eggs**

2 **tablespoons heavy cream**

1 **tablespoon orange-flavored liqueur**

1 **tablespoon sugar**

1 **teaspoon cinnamon**

2 **tablespoons butter or margarine**

½ **cup chopped banana**

½ **cup chopped seeded orange segments**

¼ **cup confectioners' sugar**

½ **cup heavy cream, stiffly beaten**

1. In medium bowl, beat together eggs, 2 tablespoons cream, the liqueur, sugar and cinnamon. Melt butter or margarine in large skillet or omelet pan over medium heat. Pour in egg mixture; reduce heat to low.

2. Cook, stirring constantly, until eggs are slightly thickened. Continue to cook without stirring until underside is golden and top surface is shiny and moist.

3. Sprinkle chopped banana and orange on the third of omelet nearest handle of pan. Using broad spatula, fold omelet into thirds, rolling to far edge of pan.

4. Place omelet on warm serving platter; sprinkle with confectioners' sugar. Serve with stiffly beaten cream.

Serves 4.

MoneySaving Tip: Eggs may just be the best all-around food bargain—no fat, no bone and plenty of nutrition. They are also one of the most adaptable foods in the world, and can be coupled with innumerable seasonings. Because eggs are so economical, you can afford to dress them up with more costly ingredients. Season scrambled eggs simply with snipped fresh or frozen chives, chopped fresh scallions, leeks or parsley. Try some omelet innovations—place some fresh-cooked vegetables in the center of a plain omelet; top the vegetables with a dollop of sour cream and add a few grains of inexpensive red caviar. Or cut up an on-sale avocado to use as a filling. The Luncheon Omelet Versailles, above, is a testament to the fact that omelets can be sweet and don't have to be relegated to the entrée category. Bring them on for a different dessert with a filling made of chopped fresh apples or pears sautéed until tender in butter and sugar, and spiced with a little grated lemon rind. A dusting of cinnamon or confectioners' sugar will make this a real treat!

Hash Brown Scramble

⅓ cup vegetable oil

3 cups frozen hash brown potatoes

1 cup chopped onion

½ cup chopped precooked ham

8 eggs

2 tablespoons heavy cream or milk

2 tablespoons grated Parmesan cheese

3 to 4 drops hot pepper sauce

¼ cup chopped parsley

1. Heat oil in large skillet over medium heat; add potatoes and onion and fry until crisp and tender, about 8 to 10 minutes, stirring occasionally. Sprinkle with ham; cook 1 minute longer.

2. In medium bowl, beat together eggs, cream or milk, grated cheese and hot pepper sauce. Pour egg mixture into skillet to flow around and under potato mixture. Cook just until eggs are set.

3. Invert onto heated serving platter; sprinkle with parsley. Cut into wedges to serve.

Serves 4.

Peppers and Scrambled Eggs

2 tablespoons butter or margarine

2 tablespoons olive oil

4 cups diced green peppers

2 cups chopped onion

8 eggs

2 tablespoons heavy cream or milk

1 teaspoon salt

¼ teaspoon pepper

1. Heat butter or margarine and oil in large skillet over low heat; add green peppers and onions and sauté until tender, about 10 minutes, stirring constantly.

2. In small bowl, beat together eggs, cream or milk, salt and pepper. Pour into skillet with peppers and onions and cook, stirring constantly, until eggs are thickened, shiny and moist. Serve over hot toast points.

Serves 4.

◯ *MoneySaving Tip:* Always leave a place in your food budget for eggs. Sometimes the variety offered in a supermarket can be confusing; the differences lie in grade and size. Standard egg sizes are jumbo, extra large, large, medium and, less frequently, small. It's worth the extra pennies to buy a dozen jumbo eggs for hard cooking, scrambling, deviling, frying and for omelets. Smaller sizes—down to medium—are fine for baked goods. Federal grades include AA and A (good for eating) and B (more economical and good for use in breads, cakes, cookies, etc.). By the way, there is no nutritional difference in white and brown eggs.

Spinach Pie

two 10-ounce packages frozen
  chopped spinach
¼ cup finely chopped onion
2 eggs, beaten
1 cup grated Parmesan cheese
1 cup ricotta or small curd
  cottage cheese
1 teaspoon salt
¼ teaspoon pepper
¼ teaspoon nutmeg

1. Cook spinach according to label directions; drain in fine sieve, pressing out all water. Place in large bowl.

2. Stir in onion, beaten eggs, Parmesan cheese and ricotta or cottage cheese; beat well. Sprinkle in salt, pepper and nutmeg; beat until well blended.

3. Pour mixture into lightly greased 9-inch pie plate. Bake at 350° F for 30 minutes. Do not overcook.

Serves 4.

Spinach-Egg Soup

½ pound sliced bacon
two 10-ounce bags fresh spinach
8 cups chicken broth or water
8 eggs, beaten
½ cup grated Parmesan cheese
1½ teaspoons salt

1. Fry bacon in large skillet over medium heat until crisp. Drain on paper towels; crumble and set aside. Reserve ¼ cup bacon fat.

2. Wash spinach well under cold running water; discard coarse stems and shred leaves finely. Place in large saucepan; cook, covered, over low heat until tender. (Water on leaves will provide enough liquid to cook spinach.) Drain in fine sieve, pressing out all water; set aside.

3. Heat chicken broth or water in large saucepan; add reserved bacon fat. Bring mixture to simmering point. Slowly pour in beaten eggs through fine strainer to form "noodles."

4. Add shredded spinach, grated cheese and salt. Heat for 2 minutes but do not boil.

Serves 4 to 6.

Cheese Crêpes

¾ cup flour

1 teaspoon baking powder

½ teaspoon salt

2 eggs

½ cup milk

½ cup water

2 tablespoons vegetable oil

one 5-ounce jar processed
cheese spread

2 tablespoons milk

2 cups grated Swiss cheese

½ teaspoon dry mustard

½ cup grated Romano or
Parmesan cheese

¼ cup butter or margarine

1. In medium bowl, sift together flour, baking powder and salt. Slowly stir in eggs, ½ cup milk and water, then beat until mixture is smooth. Chill for at least 30 minutes.

2. Make crêpes by spooning 2 tablespoons batter into a lightly oiled 6-inch skillet over medium heat. Turn skillet to coat bottom evenly with batter. Cook first side until golden, about 2 minutes; turn and cook second side for 1 minute. Keep crêpes warm; you will have 8 crêpes.

3. Combine cheese spread and 2 tablespoons milk in top of double boiler over boiling water; heat until cheese is melted. Remove from heat; stir in Swiss cheese and dry mustard.

4. Spread filling over top surface of crêpes; roll up jelly-roll fashion. Place in lightly greased 13 x 9 x 2-inch baking dish. Sprinkle with Romano or Parmesan cheese; dot with butter or margarine. Bake at 400° F for 10 minutes.

Serves 4.

Note: Unfilled crêpes may be made ahead of time, wrapped and frozen. Reheat for 10 minutes in 300° F oven to use with filling.

MoneySaving Tip: Crêpes, when made ahead and frozen, can be instantly assembled for a quick meal or impromptu entertaining, providing much style at little cost. Because their ingredients are so simple, crêpes are ideal for containing a variety of savory and sweet fillings. Leftover turkey, chicken or fish gently mixed into a delicately flavored cream sauce all make excellent fillings. Leftover vegetables, handled the same way or put into a cheese sauce, can create a different and elegant touch. Crêpes Suzette are a classic dessert, but are only the beginning as far as final-course crêpes go. Dessert fillings for crêpes can be as simple as jam or preserves. Or you can make a filling of in-season fresh fruit that you've crushed and sweetened—try strawberries or peaches. If you want to go all out, top your dessert just before serving with some whipped cream, sour cream or yogurt. Both crêpes and fillings can be made ahead and stored in the freezer.

Broccoli-Cheese Bake

1½-pound bunch fresh broccoli, or two 10-ounce packages frozen broccoli spears

¼ cup butter or margarine

2 tablespoons vegetable oil

1 cup chopped onion

6 hard-cooked eggs, sliced

one 11-ounce can Cheddar cheese soup

1 cup milk

1 cup packaged coarsely crushed herb stuffing mix

1. Wash fresh broccoli under cold running water. Trim off and discard coarse stems; cut top into large sprigs. Place in large skillet with ½ inch salted water; cover and simmer until tender, about 15 minutes. Drain. Or cook frozen broccoli according to label directions.

2. Heat 2 tablespoons of the butter or margarine and the oil in small skillet over medium heat; add onion and sauté until tender and golden, about 5 minutes.

3. Arrange broccoli over bottom of lightly greased 13 x 9 x 2-inch baking dish. Sprinkle onion over broccoli and arrange egg slices on top of vegetables.

4. In large glass measure, beat together cheese soup and milk; pour mixture over broccoli and eggs. Sprinkle with crushed stuffing mix; dot with remaining 2 tablespoons butter or margarine. Bake at 350° F for 30 minutes or until hot and bubbling.

Serves 4.

Cheese and Hash Bake

2 tablespoons butter or margarine

½ cup chopped green pepper

½ cup chopped onion

one 15-ounce can prepared corned beef hash

1½ cups grated sharp Cheddar cheese

1⅓ cups instant mashed potatoes

1. Melt butter or margarine in medium saucepan over medium heat; add green pepper and onion and sauté until tender, about 5 minutes. Remove from heat.

2. Crumble in corned beef hash; mix with fork to divide hash finely and blend with vegetables. Gently stir in 1 cup of the grated cheese. Spoon into 8 x 8 x 2-inch baking dish.

3. Prepare instant mashed potatoes according to label directions to yield 4 servings. Swirl evenly on top of hash mixture. Sprinkle with remaining cheese. Bake at 350° F for 30 minutes.

Serves 4.

Pizza Sicilian

one 16-ounce container ricotta
or small curd cottage cheese

½ cup finely chopped
precooked ham

2 tablespoons grated Parmesan
cheese

1 clove garlic, crushed

½ teaspoon salt

1 egg, beaten

two 8-ounce packages
refrigerator crescent rolls

1. Preheat oven to 400° F.

2. In medium bowl, combine ricotta or cottage cheese, ham, Parmesan cheese, garlic, salt and beaten egg. Mix to blend well; set aside.

3. Unroll 1 package crescent rolls; place dough on 15 x 9 x 1-inch jelly roll pan. Press to seal perforations and make one sheet of dough. Spread cheese mixture over dough to within ½ inch of edges.

4. Unroll second package crescent rolls on lightly floured board; press to seal perforations. Using rolling pin, lift second sheet of dough and cover cheese mixture. Dampen all edges and press with fork to seal well. Bake for 12 to 15 minutes, until crust is deep golden brown and filling is hot.

Serves 4.

Fontina-Tomato Fondue

1 clove garlic, split

2 tablespoons butter or
margarine

1 pound fontina cheese, cubed

1 cup dry white wine

one 10¾-ounce can tomato soup

2 tablespoons flour

1 loaf crusty Italian or French
bread, cubed

1. Rub bottom and sides of medium saucepan well with garlic. Add butter or margarine and melt over low heat. Add cheese and wine; continue to heat, stirring constantly, until cheese is melted.

2. In small bowl, blend together soup and flour. Stir into cheese mixture. Cook, stirring constantly, until mixture simmers.

3. Place saucepan on tripod over canned heat source. Serve with cubes of crusty bread for dipping.

Serves 4.

Cheese-Stuffed Potatoes

4 large baking potatoes
1 tablespoon vegetable oil
½ pound sliced bacon
½ cup butter or margarine
½ cup heavy cream
2 tablespoons grated onion
1 teaspoon salt
¼ teaspoon pepper
1 cup grated sharp Cheddar cheese

1. Scrub potatoes well; pat dry. Prick all over with fork and rub lightly with oil. Bake at 450° F for 1 hour or until easily pierced with a skewer. Cool potatoes enough to handle.

2. Meanwhile, fry bacon in large skillet over medium heat until crisp. Drain on paper towels; crumble and set aside.

3. Cut a ½-inch slice from one long side of each potato to form a lid. Using a teaspoon, scoop out pulp, leaving a shell ¼ inch thick.

4. Place pulp in large bowl with butter or margarine, cream, onion, salt and pepper. Mash together or beat with electric mixer at high speed until smooth.

5. Stir in grated cheese and crumbled bacon; mix to blend well. Fill potato shells with mixture. Bake at 350° F for 30 minutes.

Serves 4.

Potato Puff

2 cups instant mashed potatoes
one 8-ounce jar sharp processed cheese spread
3 eggs, slightly beaten
2 tablespoons grated onion
¼ teaspoon pepper

1. Prepare instant mashed potatoes according to label directions to yield 6 servings.

2. Beat in cheese spread until melted and well mixed. Beat in slightly beaten eggs, onion and pepper.

3. Spoon into lightly greased 1-quart casserole or soufflé dish. Bake at 350° F for 30 minutes or until golden and puffy.

Serves 4.

Tropical Fruit and Cheese Mold

one 16-ounce can mixed fruit
salad

one 15½-ounce can crushed
pineapple

one 3-ounce package lemon-
flavored gelatin

1 cup boiling water

one 16-ounce container large
curd cottage cheese, drained

1. Drain juices from fruit salad and pineapple into glass measure; reserve 1 cup fruit juice. Set fruits aside.

2. In medium bowl, dissolve gelatin in boiling water; stir in reserved fruit juice. Chill until mixture is consistency of unbeaten egg whites, about 30 minutes.

3. Fold in drained fruit salad, pineapple and cottage cheese. Pour into 1½-quart mold or 8 x 8 x 2-inch baking dish. Chill until firm, at least 1 hour.

Serves 4 to 6.

Index

Acorn squash, sausage-stuffed, 44, **66**
Almond chicken and rice, 94
Artichokes, turkey casserole and, 95

Beans, 111–113
  baked, with sausage, 45
  black, Brazilian, 111
  black, soup, 111
  lentil soup, 113
  lentils and sausages, baked, 113
  lima-tomato soup, hearty, 112
  pasta with, 118
  and rice, Jamaican style, 120
  three-bean salad, 112
Beef, 7–32
  Burgundy, budget, 16
  California, 12
  casserole, and corn, 24
  casserole, corned beef, 32
  casserole, farm-style, 25
  casserole, rice-kraut, 26
  casserole, and shells, 28
  celery-cream, with almonds, 30
  curry-ginger, 15
  goulash, and onion, 15
  London broil, marinated, 14
  meat loaf, herb and tomato, 22
  meat roll, stuffed pinwheel, 23
  moussaka, speedy, 26
  and noodles Hungarian, 27
  pie, and cheese, 23
  pot roast, Belgian, 9
  pot roast, wine-tender, 9
  rice and macaroni Italian with, 28
  rolls, Italian-style, 13
  sandwiches, Sloppy Joe pocket, 20
  sauerbraten, 10
  short ribs, in barbecue sauce, 17
  skillet casserole, Chinese, 24
  skillet casserole, Mexican-style, 25

Beef (continued)
  skillet casserole, with noodles, 27
  soup, and barley, 18
  stew, Vincenza, 17
  in stuffed cabbage, 31
  in stuffed eggplant, 30
  taco con carne, 29
  see also Burgers, beef; Liver, beef;
    Meatballs; Steak
Brains beurre noir, 81
Burgers, beef:
  Mexicana, 19
  pepper, 20
  smothered blue cheese, 19
  Wellington, 29
Burgers, sausage, Creole style, 49

Cabbage:
  caraway, pork chops and, 37
  stuffed, 31
Casseroles:
  beef and corn, 24
  beef and noodle skillet, 27
  beef-and-shells, 28
  Chinese beef skillet, 24
  corned beef, 32
  farm-style beef, 25
  frank and kraut, 51
  ham and pasta, savory, 43
  Mexican-style skillet, 25
  pork and rice, 39
  rice-kraut, 26
  sausage and eggplant, 46
  sausage and ziti, 48
  savory frankfurter, 50
  scrapple, 54
  Swiss cheese and ham, 43
  three country, 11
  tuna and biscuit, 106
  tuna-green bean, 104
  turkey-artichoke, 95

Cheese:
  crêpes, 128
  fondue, fontina-tomato, 130
  hash bake and, 129
  herb cream, noodles with, 117
  pizza Sicilian, 130
  potatoes stuffed with, 131
  and savory beef pie, 23
  and spinach stuffed shells, 119
  Swiss and ham casserole, 43
  three-cheese spinach noodles, **71**,
    117
  and tropical fruit mold, 132
  tuna quiche with, 106
Chicken, 85–94
  almond, and rice, 94
  barbecue-baked, 87
  breasts, crisp oven-fried, 93
  deviled, 87
  drumsticks, Shanghai, 94
  gratiné, crisp, 92
  Juliet, 88
  luau, 88
  in mushroom-shrimp sauce, 92
  roast, herb, 86
  roast, lemon, 85
  roast, with orange rice stuffing, 85
  roast, peachy, **69**, 86
  rolls, cordon bleu, 91
  simple savory, 89
  skillet, and tarragon rice, 89
  Spanish style, 90
  tangy yogurt, 93
  in white wine, 90
Chicken liver:
  omelet, 77
  piquant, and chestnuts, 78
Clams Ramon, 108
Cod Portugaise, stuffed, 99
Corn and beef casserole, 24
Corned beef casserole, 32

Crêpes, cheese, 128
Croquettes, ham, 42

Eggplant:
   casserole, with sausage, 46
   moussaka, speedy, 26
   stuffed, 30
Eggs, 123–127
   Chantilly, 123
   chicken liver omelet, 77
   double creamy, 123
   frittata, sausage and, 124
   hash brown scramble, 126
   herb sausage and, 45
   luncheon omelet Versailles, 125
   pepperoni omelet, 49
   and peppers, scrambled, 126
   ratatouille omelet, **72,** 124
   soup, with spinach, 127
   spinach pie, 127

Fish, 98–108
   cod Portugaise, stuffed, 99
   in cream-wine sauce, 100
   fillets, savory baked, 100
   flounder, broiled crisp, 98
   flounder in lemon wine sauce, 98
   haddock, creamy, in celery sauce,
     99
   salmon mousse pie, 103
   sardine supper, 102
   see also Seafood; Tuna
Fishburgers, 101
Flounder:
   broiled crisp, 98
   in lemon wine sauce, 98
Fondue, fontina-tomato, 130
Frankfurters:
   casserole, with sauerkraut, 51
   casserole, savory, 50
   Hawaiian, 50
   mash, 51

Goulash, beef and onion, 15

Haddock, creamy, in celery sauce,
   99
Ham, 41–43
   baked, crusty, 41
   casserole, and pasta, 43

Ham *(continued)*
   casserole, and Swiss cheese, 43
   croquettes, 42
   loaf, baked, 41
   roast, curried, 41
   shank dinner, boiled, 42
Hamburgers, *see* Burgers
Hash and cheese, baked, 129
Hot dogs, *see* Frankfurters

Kidneys:
   and onions in wine, 81
   stew, with mushrooms, 80
Kielbasa and hot potato salad, 52
Knockwurst in beer, 52

Lamb, 61–64
   shanks, Greek style, 64, **67**
   stew, home style, 63
   stew, curried, 63
Lamb chops:
   English style, 61
   marinated, and tomatoes, 62
   orange pan-broiled, 62
Lentil soup, 113
Lentils and sausage, baked, 113
Liver, beef:
   baked, mustardy, 76
   cutlets, 75
   Italian style, 75
Liver, calves':
   au poivre, **68,** 77
   Italian style, 75
   sherried, 76
Liver, chicken, *see* Chicken liver
London broil, marinated, 14

Macaroni (pasta), 114–119
   angry, 114
   bake, 115
   with beef and rice, Italian, 28
   casserole, Saturday lunch beef-
     and-shells, 28
   casserole, savory ham and, 43
   casserole, ziti and sausage, 48
   linguine in garlic-clam sauce, 114
   pie, 115
   rigatoni Castagna style, 118
   shells stuffed with cheese and
     spinach, 119

Macaroni *(continued)*
   spaghetti carbonara, 119
   see also Noodles
Meatballs:
   Simple Simon, 21
   Susan's Swedish, 21
   sweet-sour, 22
Meat loaf, herb and tomato, 22
Meat roll, stuffed pinwheel, 23
Moussaka, speedy, 26
Mushrooms:
   breast of veal stuffed with, 59
   kidney stew with, 80
   veal stew with, 59
Mussels, iced marinated, **70,** 107

Noodles:
   Alsatian skillet dinner, 116
   and bacon bake, 116
   with beans, 118
   with herb cream cheese, 117
   Hungarian, with beef, 27
   skillet casserole, beef and, 27
   three-cheese spinach, **71,** 117
   see also Macaroni

Oxtail soup, 18

Pasta, *see* Macaroni; Noodles
Peachy roast chicken, **69,** 86
Pepperoni omelet, 49
Peppers:
   pork chops and, 38
   savory stuffed, 47
   scrambled eggs and, 126
   skillet, with sausage, 47
Pies:
   beef and cheese, savory, 23
   macaroni, 115
   salmon mousse, 103
   spinach, 127
   veal, creamy, 60
Pizza Sicilian, 130
Pork, 35–40
   casserole, and rice, 39
   rib ends, spicy, 40
   see also Ham; Sausage; *and specific*
     pork dishes
Porkburger-apple-potato platter, 48

Pork chops:
  caraway cabbage and, 37
  Italian style, 37
  parmigiana, 38
  peppers and, 38
  sweet-sour, 39
  vino bianco, 40
Pork roast:
  with onions and potatoes, 35
  with sauerkraut, 35
  spiced, 35
Pork shoulder:
  glazed, and curried fruit, 36
  herbed, 36
Potatoes, cheese-stuffed, 131
Potato puff, 131
Potato salad, hot, with kielbasa, 52
Pot roast:
  Belgian beef, 9
  wine-tender, 9

Quiche, tuna-cheese, 106

Ratatouille omelet, **72,** 124
Rib ends, spicy, 40
Rice, 120–122
  with almond chicken, 94
  and beans Jamaican style, 120
  with beef and macaroni, Italian, 28
  casserole, with kraut, 26
  casserole, with pork, 39
  Genoese, 120
  Italian style, 121
  orange, chicken stuffed with, 85
  salad Provençal, 122
  tarragon, skillet chicken and, 89
  tomatoes stuffed with, 122
Rigatoni Castagna style, 118

Salads:
  potato, hot, with kielbasa, 52
  rice Provençal, 122
  squid, vinaigrette, 102
  three-bean, traditional, 112
  turkey Waldorf, 96
Salmon mousse pie, 103
Sandwiches:
  open-face wurst, 53

Sandwiches *(continued)*
  pocket, Sloppy Joe, 20
  savory scrapple, 53
Sardine supper, 102
Sauerbraten, old-world, 10
Sauerkraut:
  casserole, frank and, 51
  casserole, with rice, 26
  pork roast with, 35
Sausage:
  acorn squash stuffed with, 44, **66**
  Alsace style, 44
  baked beans and, 45
  baked lentils and, 113
  burgers, Creole style, 49
  casserole, with eggplant, 46
  casserole, with ziti, 48
  and egg frittata, 124
  herb, and egg supper, 45
  Italian, and onions, 46
  in savory stuffed peppers, 47
  skillet, with peppers, 47
  wurst (Braunschweiger), in open-face sandwiches, 53
Scrapple:
  casserole, 54
  sandwiches, 53
Seafood, 98–108
  clams Ramon, 108
  mussels, iced marinated, **70,** 107
  squid salad vinaigrette, 102
  see also Fish; Tuna
Short ribs in barbecue sauce, 17
Soup:
  beef and barley, hearty, 18
  black bean, 111
  lentil, 113
  lima-tomato, hearty, 112
  oxtail, 18
  spinach-egg, 127
  turkey, hearty homemade, 97
Spaghetti carbonara, 119
Spinach:
  breast of veal stuffed with, 58
  noodles, three-cheese, **71,** 117
  pie, 127
  shells stuffed with cheese and, 119
  soup, with eggs, 127
Squash, acorn, sausage-stuffed, 44, **66**

Squid salad vinaigrette, 102
Steak:
  flank, stuffed, 14
  pizzaiola, chuck, 10
  round, braised, 12
  skillet, sauté, 11, **65**

Taco con carne, 29
Tomatoes:
  marinated lamb chops and, 62
  rice-stuffed, 122
  tuna-stuffed, 107
Tongue:
  with mustard sauce, 80
  with raisin sour sauce, 79
  with wine sauce, 78
Tripe:
  marinara, 82
  Milanese, 82
Tropical fruit and cheese mold, 132
Tuna, 103–107
  casserole, and biscuit, 106
  casserole, with green beans, 104
  deviled, 104
  hot pot, crispy, 103
  quiche, with cheese, 106
  Savoy, 105
  tetrazzini, 105
  tomatoes stuffed with, 107
Turkey, 95–97
  casserole, with artichokes, 95
  continental, 96
  drumsticks, oven-baked, 95
  goodbye, 97
  soup, hearty homemade, 97
  Waldorf salad, 96

Veal, 57–61
  breast of, mushroom-stuffed, 59
  breast of, spinach-stuffed, 58
  breast of, stuffed, 58
  pies, creamy, 60
  polpetti, 61
  stew, with mushrooms, 59
  stew paprikash, 60
Veal chops:
  cordon bleu, easy, 57
  herb, crisp-baked, 57